Introducing

Microsoft Access 2.0

FOR

WINDOWS

TIMOTHY TRAINOR & JEFFREY STIPES

Introducing

Microsoft Access 2.0

FOR

WINDOWS

McGRAW-HILL

New York St. Louis San Francisco Auckland Bogotá Caracas
Lisbon London Madrid Mexico Milan Montreal New Delhi
Paris San Juan Singapore Sydney Tokyo Toronto

McGRAW-HILL
San Francisco, California

Introducing Microsoft Access 2.0 for Windows

1 2 3 4 5 6 7 8 9 0   SEM SEM   9 0 9 8 7 6 5 4

ISBN 0-07-065257-0

Sponsoring Editor: Roger L. Howell
Editorial Assistant: Rhonda Sands
Production Supervisor: Richard DeVitto
Project Manager: Books International
Interior Design: Gary Palmatier
Cover Designer: Christy Butterfield
Printer: Semline, Inc.

Library of Congress Catalog Card Number 93-78714

Contents

DATABASE

3   Creating Reports and Two Table Queries

51

4 Enhancing Database Applications

75

DATABASE

Introduction

![bar]

INTRODUCING ACCESS 2.0 FOR WINDOWS

Database programs are used to organize, store, manipulate, and retrieve important facts and figures. They simplify the mechanics of producing professional-looking data entry screens and reports. Databases can be used to organize inventory, customer lists, transactions, and other business or personal data.

Introducing Access 2.0 for Windows gives you the knowledge and expertise to develop simple to complex queries, data entry forms, and reports using integrated databases. This tutorial helps the user become comfortable with the essentials of Microsoft's Access 2.0 for Windows and feel confident exploring the program's capabilities.

Using This Module

This section is designed to assist you in completing each lesson. Lessons begin with goals listed under the heading Objectives. Key terms are introduced in ***bold italics*** type; text to be typed by the user is shown in **bold**. Also keep in mind the following:

■ This symbol is used to indicate the user's action.

▶ *This symbol is used to indicate the screen's response.*

Alternative: Presents an alternative keystroke or icon "shortcut."

NOTE: This format is for important user notes or tips.

PRACTICE TIME

These brief drills allow the user to practice features previously discussed. Each lesson assumes all previous Practice Times have been completed.

Finally, a series of projects, a command summary, and a glossary of key terms are found at the end of the book.

BEFORE YOU START

Access 2.0 operates within Microsoft's graphical user interface called Windows. Many operating procedures are common to all Windows-compatible software packages and Intel-based microcomputers. We are assuming you are familiar with the following procedures:

- Turning on your computer, printer, and screen
- Using a mouse and keyboard
- Formatting a disk
- Displaying a disk's directory
- Copying files to another disk
- Loading a formatted disk (referred to as the data disk) into a disk drive
- Activating Microsoft's Windows graphical user interface
- Working within Window's desktop

If any of these assumptions are incorrect, ask your instructor for help.

To use this book, you need Access 2.0 for Windows installed in the Microsoft Windows 3.1 operating environment. In addition, you must have a formatted floppy disk containing data supplied by your instructor. A standard hardware configuration with floppy disk (drive A), mouse, and printer installed through Windows is also assumed.

The data disk contains several tables used in Lessons 3 and 4. These files are supplied by your instructor to reduce the amount of data entry necessary to complete these lessons.

In some situations, you will be working with a personal computer that is connected to other computers in a Local Area Network or LAN. You will need additional information concerning commands for linking your computer into the network. Use the space below to write out each step.

Printer type: _____

Access disk drive: _____

LAN procedures: _____

_____

_____

_____

_____

_____

_____

_____

DATABASE

ACKNOWLEDGMENTS

We would like to acknowledge the contribution of the following people who reviewed the manuscript:

Louis Adelson, Clarion University

Carolyn Alexander, Phillips County Community College

Barbara Felty, Harrisburg Area Community College

Lanny Felty, Harrisburg Area Community College

Krystal Scott, Oklahoma Baptist University

Paula Thompson, Delta State University

F. Stuart Wells, Ph.D., Tennessee Technological University

We would also like to thank the entire Microcomputer Applications Using Windows 3.1 class at the 1994 National Computer Educator's Institute who class-tested this text in a preliminary form.

Tim Trainor
Jeff Stipes

LESSON

Creating Database Tables and Forms

OBJECTIVES

Upon completion of the material presented in this lesson, you should understand the following aspects of Access:

- ❏ **Launching Access**
- ❏ **Using database terminology**
- ❏ **Setting up new database**
- ❏ **Creating data tables**
- ❏ **Locating data values within a table**
- ❏ **Setting up a data entry form**
- ❏ **Saving data tables and forms on disk**
- ❏ **Printing data**
- ❏ **Exiting Access**

DATABASE

OVERVIEW

In our modern society, there is a growing need to manage data. A *database management system (DBMS)* is a software tool that permits people to use a computer's ability to store, retrieve, modify, organize, and display key facts. Stored data is an extremely valuable asset for any person or organization using a computer system. People rely on organized data in the form of telephone books, airline schedules, meeting agendas, etc., to conduct their daily activities.

DBMS helps organize data based on the user's need; for instance, a video store might organize data concerning video tape rentals.

- Letters, numbers, and special symbols are the simplest forms of data people use. These characters make up a customer's name or the title of a movie. A DBMS needs to know what type of character combinations to expect. You might want it to limit acceptable characters to numbers or valid dates.

- When characters are combined together, they form data *fields.* Fields are the facts that can be transformed into information through processing. For each video tape the computer would store a field for the movie's title, release date, replacement cost, etc. Data fields are given generic *field names* as a means of reference, like Video Title field or Last Name field. Data management software will also require that each field be identified by type. Common field types would include text, number, date/time, or yes/no.

- Collections of related fields form records. A *record* describes a person, place, object, or event. In the video store rental system, the data about each customer would make up a customer record. There also would be a record for each video tape and each time a tape is rented.

- *Tables* contain groups of records related by a common theme. For example, video tape records would be in a different table from the customer records. The table that contains all video tape records would be called the inventory table. All the customer records become the customer table.

The power and sophistication of data management software varies greatly. The software dictates whether data in tables are independent or can be integrated. The more sophisticated DBMS, for example, Microsoft's Access 2.0 for Windows, can integrate data from several tables into a *relational database.* As shown in Figure 1-1, a relational DBMS can retrieve and integrate data from several tables at the same time.

The video store could integrate data from the inventory and customer tables. When customers rent a video, a store employee scans the customer number from their ID card. The DBMS then uses this number as a *key* field to uniquely identify the customer's record. The record is retrieved from disk to extract a name and other data from the customer table. The same procedure is used to retrieve the video's tape number from the inventory table. As a result, only the customer number and tape number are entered

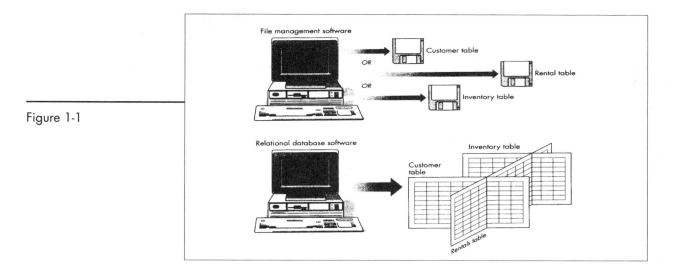

Figure 1-1

to rent a video. A less sophisticated file management system would also require entering the movie's title along with the customer's name, address, and telephone number each time tapes are rented.

Each DBMS package has special features and specific approaches to database development and management. However, the basic operating procedures for any database management system take one of two approaches. The first approach is to initiate action through a series of key words or commands. Users enter commands from the keyboard like "Create CUSTOMER.DBF" or "Display Last-Name, Telephone When State = "MI"." These command-driven packages often have special menu-driven help screens for beginners. Other database management systems rely on menus and icons (pictures) that depict the action in which users wish to engage. Access falls into this category with its graphical user interface that is compatible with Microsoft's Windows operating environment. Tables are created and accessed by selecting the appropriate icon or menu option.

STARTING ACCESS

Before starting Access, turn on your computer system and start Microsoft's Windows program.

- ■ Turn on your computer, screen, and printer.

- ■ If necessary, link to a local area network.

- ■ Place your formatted data disk into a disk drive.

- ■ Start the Windows program.

- ■ Make sure the Program Manager is the only window displayed on the screen.

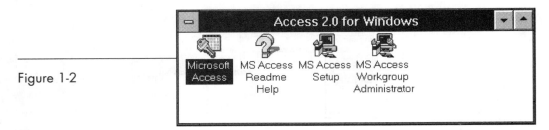

Figure 1-2

- Maximize the Program Manager window.

- Double-click on the Access for Windows or Microsoft Office group icon, 🔲 or 🔲 . Your computer system might use another label for this group icon. Check with your instructor for your particular setup.

  ▶ *The installation procedure for Access creates a program group which includes icons for Microsoft Access and associated utility programs, as shown in Figure 1-2.*

NOTE: If you do not double-click fast enough, Windows displays the control menu. When this happens, just click on the <u>R</u>estore option or press R to launch Access.

- Launch Access by double-clicking on the Microsoft Access icon, 🔲 .

  ▶ *After the logo screen the Access application window opens. This window may display the Access Cue Cards dialog box, as shown at the bottom of Figure 1-3.*

The Cue Cards option offers step-by-step instructions for tasks you are performing. It is one of several types of help provided by Access. Other types of online help will be discussed at a later time. If the Cue Cards dialog box is displayed, you can close it. You will not be using Cue Cards in this book.

- If the Cue Cards dialog box is open, select the Don't display this startup card again check box and double-click on the control box.

  Alternative: Press ALT+F4.

  ▶ *The Access application window is displayed, as shown at the top of Figure 1-3.*

- Maximize the Access window.

THE ACCESS APPLICATION WINDOW

The Access window contains the same basic elements of any application window. As shown in Figure 1-4, a *title bar* along the top identifies the

Figure 1-3

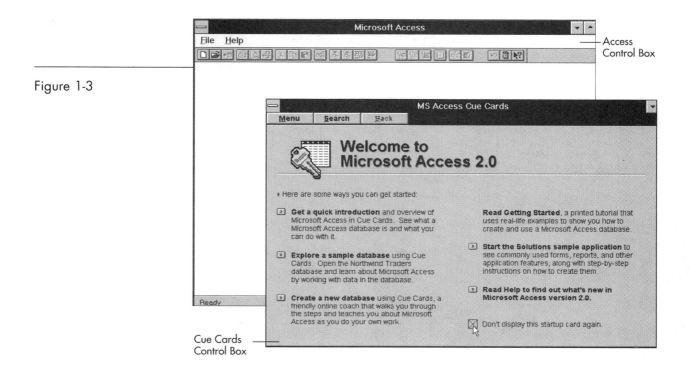

Access
Control Box

Cue Cards
Control Box

DATABASE

application (Microsoft Access) and the *menu bar* underneath it offers *drop-down menus*, in this case File and Help. Access commands are activated by clicking on the desired menu name or by holding down the Alt key and pressing the key of the underlined letter in the menu name. For example, holding down the Alt key and pressing F, ALT+F, opens the File menu. When a menu is selected, the available commands appear in the drop down menu. Dimmed menu options cannot be activated.

Don't be fooled by this simple layout. The Access desktop comes alive with options once you open a database.

Tool Bar

Beneath the menu bar is the **tool bar** which contains a row of **tool buttons** that you can click to quickly perform Access's most commonly used commands. Tool buttons exist for copying, printing, saving files, etc. Access provides a brief explanation of each button in the tool bar when you move the pointer over the button and pause for a moment.

■   Move the pointer over each button and pause.

▶   *A description of each button's function appears under the pointer and in the status bar.*

NOTE: If the descriptions *do not* appear, press ESC and try again.

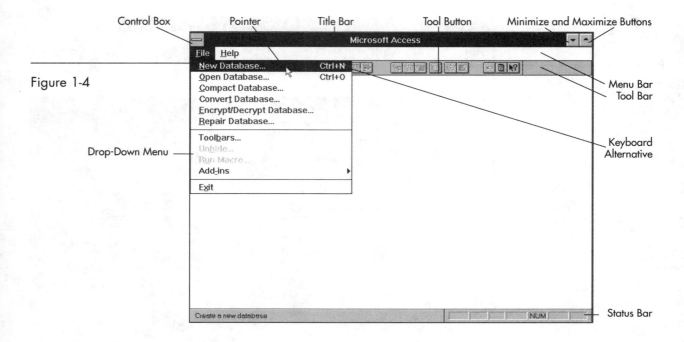

Figure 1-4

Status Bar

The ***status bar***, found at the bottom of every Access window (see Figure 1-4), also displays information about the highlighted menu option. In addition, this area is used to display input prompts. When questions occur, glance down to this screen location to see if a helpful description or example is provided.

■   Click on the File menu name and hold down the mouse button.

▶   *File menu opens, as shown in Figure 1-4.*

■   Drag the mouse pointer along the menu bar and down the menus as they open.

▶   *The status bar displays descriptions of each option as the pointer passes over it.*

■   Move pointer into an open area of the screen and release the mouse button.

CREATING A NEW DATABASE

Tables, data entry forms, reports, and other objects you use Access to create are placed in a database. The design and development of a usable database are somewhat like building a new house. The architect must understand the needs of the home owner before a compatible design can be achieved. To

Figure 1-5

CUSTOMER TABLE

Customer Number	First Name	Last Name	Address	City	State/Prov	Zip/Postal Code
881464	Alice	Harris	734 Mercury Drive	Hackley	MI	49442
882882	John	Wilson	12456 East Stone R	Grand Lake	MI	49457
884317	George	Miller	789 Robins Road	Wilson Park	MI	49480
886951	Sandy	Davis	4533 Ritter Drive	Hackley	MI	49442
891254	Todd	Evans	1351 Willow Lane	Hackley	MI	49441
894239	Mary	Richardson	1728 Apple Avenue	Grand Lake	MI	49457
896444	Frank	Stevens	96381 Pinewood	Hackley	MI	49442
897062	Charles	Billings	1879 Strong	Wilson Park	MI	49480
898837	Carol	Taylor	8845 Garfield Road	Grand Lake	MI	49457
899111	Roxanne	Little	3657 Wilson	Hackley	MI	49442
913271	Bill	Alberts	682 Williams	Wilson Park	MI	49480
915968	Martha	Young	226 E. 120th	Hackley	MI	49443
916389	Judy	Harris	3226 Wolf Lake Roc	Hackley	MI	49441
917222	Alan	McCarthy	17984 Cove Harbor	Hackley	MI	49441
919977	Dan	Kamp	456 State	Hackley	MI	49443

Customer Number	Tape Number	Date Out	Date In			
881464	16828	8/8/92	8/9/92	d Lake	MI	49457
881464	44332	8/19/92	8/20/92	kley	MI	49442
881464	47739	8/30/92		on Park	MI	49480
881464	48419	8/9/92	8/10/92	d Lake	MI	49457
881464	48800	8/12/92	8/13/92	kley	MI	49441
881464	50613	8/5/92	6/6/92			
882882	40013	8/22/92	8/23/92			
882882	46599	8/16/92	8/17/92			
882882	48422	8/18/92	8/19/92			
882882	48799	8/3/92	8/4/92			
882882	48801	8/21/92				
882882	63456	8/11/92	8/12/92			
884239	47315	8/24/92	8/25/92			
884317	16828	8/15/92	8/17/92			
884317	37612	8/8/92	8/9/92			
884317						
884317						
884317						
886951						
886951						

RENTALS TABLE

Tape Number	Movie ID	Available	Purchase Date	Purchase Price
16827	101	Y	1/5/93	$39.75
16828	101	Y	1/5/93	$39.75
23184	113	Y	3/5/93	$42.85
23185	113	Y	3/5/93	$42.85
23186	113	Y	3/5/93	$42.85
23187	113	Y	10/5/93	$42.85
37611	114	N	3/17/93	$35.60
37612	114	Y	3/17/93	$35.60
39955	111	Y	4/2/93	$29.95
39956	111	Y	4/2/93	$29.95
40012	102	Y	3/27/88	$39.75
40013	102	Y	3/27/88	$39.75
40014	102	Y	3/27/88	$39.75
42137	109	Y	7/9/93	$35.60
42138	109	Y	7/9/93	$35.60
42139		Y		
43765				
43766				
44331				
44332				
46130				
46131				
46599				
47314				
47315				

INVENTORY TABLE

MOVIES TABLE

Movie ID	Movie Title	Production Company	Category	Release Date	Rating
101	Casablanca	Warner Bros.	O	9/11/42	None
102	African Queen	20th Century-Fox	O	10/12/51	None
103	Dirty Harry	Warner Bros.	A	3/18/71	R
104	Star Wars	20th Century-Fox	S	5/25/77	PG
105	Friday the 13th	Paramount	H	1/9/80	R
106	Star Trek	Paramount	S	12/20/79	G
107	Raiders of the Lost Ark	Paramount	A	7/23/81	G
108	Ghostbusters	Columbia	C	7/16/84	PG
109	Jaws	Universal	H	4/20/75	R
111	The Godfather	Paramount	D	10/11/72	R
112	Die Hard	20th Century-Fox	A	6/30/88	R
113	Ghost	Paramount	D	2/24/90	PG13
114	Pretty Woman	Touchstone	C	5/20/90	R
115	Dances with Wolves	Orion	A	11/9/90	PG13
116	Jurassic Park	Amblin	A	5/1/93	PG13
117	Adventures of Your Name	Your Course Name	A	11/27/95	PG
118	Your selection #1	Touchstone	D	2/4/89	G
119	Your selection #2	Orion	A	7/9/83	PG

make this point in regards to database applications, we will take a closer look at the needs of our local video store—Boomtown Video Rentals.

The video store's relational database, called VIDSTORE, would use several integrated tables (see Figure 1-5). The CUSTOMER table maintains the names, addresses, telephone, and rental status of the people with whom we do business. A unique customer number is assigned to everyone and serves as a key field. A separate RENTALS table tracks each customer transaction (rental). The INVENTORY table lists each tape carried by the store.

To reduce the data redundancy caused by stocking several copies of the same movie, the title and other information common to several tapes is kept in a separate MOVIES table. The MOVIES and INVENTORY tables are linked by the movie's ID number. As a result, we can carry three copies of the movie *ET*, but we only need to include the title, release date, category (adventure, comedy, horror, etc.), and other related information once in the MOVIES table. Three different tape numbers are assigned to the tapes and become independent records in the INVENTORY table.

Working Disk Drive

In this lesson you will create the VIDSTORE database and MOVIES table. The MOVIES table is then loaded with some of your favorite movie titles. You need to designate a **working disk drive** for Access to store the VIDSTORE database. When using this tutorial, you should always select the drive into which you placed your data disk as the working drive. The STUDENT database with CUSTOMER, RENTALS, and INVENTORY tables should have been provided on your data disk. In later lessons you will integrate these tables into the VIDSTORE database.

■   Open the <u>F</u>ile menu.

■   Select the <u>N</u>ew Database command, as shown in Figure 1-4.

> *Alternative:*   Press ALT+F, then N, or use the new database tool button, ⬜ .

▶   *The New Database dialog box is displayed.*

At this time a formatted data disk with the STUDENT database should already be inserted into the computer's disk drive. If you do not have a data disk with this database, ask your instructor for a copy before continuing. In this tutorial, examples will always use drive A.

■   Click on the Dri<u>v</u>es down-arrow button.

▶   *The Drives list box opens.*

■   Select the drive letter for the disk drive holding your data disk.

▶   *The Directories list box displays all the directories currently on your data disk. If you need to specify a directory, do so by clicking on the directory name.*

■   Click in the File <u>N</u>ame text box.

▶   *An I-beam pointer appears in text box.*

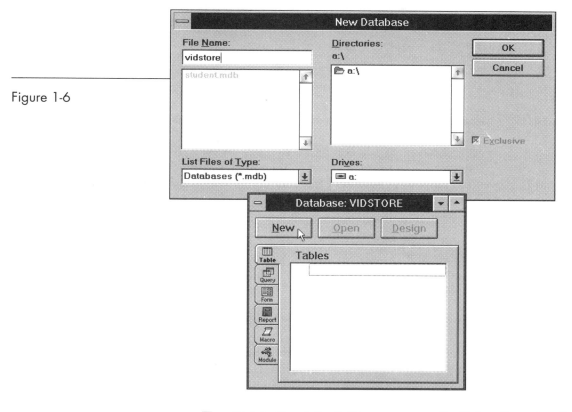

Figure 1-6

- Delete the default filename, usually db1.mdb, using the BACKSPACE and DELETE keys.

- Type **vidstore,** as shown at the top of Figure 1-6, and complete the command by clicking on OK or pressing ENTER.

  ▶ *The VIDSTORE database window opens, as shown at the bottom of Figure 1-6.*

Access automatically adds the filename extension .MDB to all database files.

CREATING A DATA TABLE

Next, the MOVIES table needs to be added to the VIDSTORE database. The Table button should currently be active and Tables displayed on top of the list box as shown at the bottom of Figure 1-6. Other objects, like forms and reports, are created or opened by selecting the appropriate button found on the left side of the database dialog box. The buttons on the top—New, Open, and Design—initiate the desired actions.

- Select the New button.

> ▶ *The New Table dialog box is displayed, containing the Table Wizards, New Table, and Cancel buttons.*

■ Select the New Table button.

> ▶ *The Table 1 window opens. Figure 1-7 shows how this window will be filled out.*

Data Types

The MOVIES table contains five fields for every record. We need to establish generic field names for each field. At the same time Access needs to know the field type, size, and whether the field is used as a key.

■ Type **Movie ID** in the first row under Field Name and press ENTER.

> ▶ *Text in the Data Type column is highlighted.*

NOTE: Data type options are displayed by clicking on the down arrow button, as shown in Figure 1-7.

Access uses 8 different field types:

- *Text* fields contain letters, numbers, special symbols (!,@,#,$,%), or any of the standard ASCII characters used by personal computers. These alphanumeric fields are limited to a maximum length of 255 characters. When in doubt it is best to designate a field as text. Telephone numbers, social security numbers, and similar fields that appear to be numeric often include hyphens and spaces which make them text.

- *Memo* fields are reserved for text fields that exceed the limit of 255 characters. These fields can be up to 32,000 characters long. Like text fields, memo fields can contain any combination of characters.

- *Number* fields only contain numbers and an optional decimal point or minus sign. You should use number field types when the field will be used in numeric calculations. For example, Hours Worked and Pay Rate would be number fields because they are used to compute a person's wages.

- *Date/Time* fields contain any valid date or time. Several date formats are available from the long date (July 9, 1994), to the medium date format (9-Jul-94) and short date (7/9/94). The time format appears as 2:24 P.M. Access checks each entry for validity. If you enter an invalid date or time, an error dialog box displays the message "The value you entered isn't appropriate for this field."

- *Currency* fields are special number fields that are preset to show two decimal places and a leading $ sign.

- *Counter* fields contain integer (whole) numbers that Access automatically increments as you add records. These fields could be used

Figure 1-7

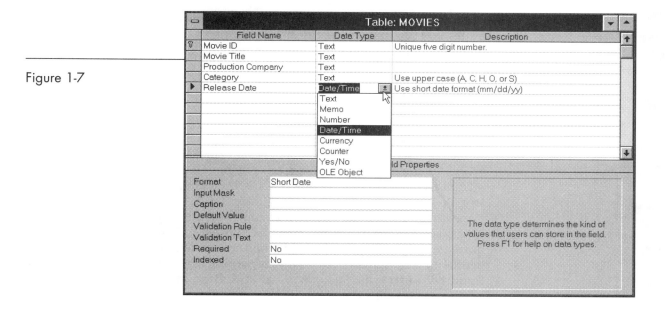

to increment the customer number as new customers are added to a table.

- *Yes/No* fields are set to one of two values. You could create a Yes/No field in each inventory record to indicate whether a tape is available for a customer to rent. In this case, "Yes" means the tape is in the store and available to rent while "No" means the tape is out or unusable for some reason.

- *OLE* (Object Linking and Embedding) fields take advantage of features associated with the Windows operating environment. An OLE field can contain an object, for instance, 50 pages of text or a complete spreadsheet, that is created and maintain by other software. Any changes to the object after it is installed in the Access table are automatically updated. This field type is limited to advanced applications.

Enter each field name, type, and size as described. Press the Enter key after each entry. The Movie ID is the key field and must be the first field.

NOTE: Fields can be inserted or deleted if necessary. Highlighting any part of a field definition and pressing the Ins key will insert a new field. Likewise, pressing the two key combination of Ctrl + Del will delete a field entry.

- ■ Press ENTER to select Text as the data type.

  ▶ *A flashing cursor moves to the Description column.*

- ■ Type **Unique five digit number.**

This description will appear in the status bar of any data entry form using this field. Next, to save storage space, you need to change the maximum field size from 50 characters to 5. This still leaves the store room for 99,999 separate movie titles.

■   Click behind 50 in the Field Size box.

■   Use BACKSPACE to delete the 0.

▶   *Field Size is 5.*

Primary Key

While Access does not require a table to have a key field, there are several advantages to designating Movie ID as the **primary key.** Since a primary key is unique to each record in the table, Access does not permit duplicates. If two records had the same key, the key field could no longer be used to identify either record. Another advantage is that Access automatically creates an index using the key field. Indexes help speed up access to data. This is especially important when using large tables with hundreds of records. Records are always displayed in the key field order.

■   Click on Movie ID.

▶   *A flashing cursor appears in the field name.*

■   Click on the key button (🔑) in the Tool bar.

▶   *A key is inserted in front of the black pointer (current field indicator) to the left of the field name.*

PRACTICE TIME 1-1

Using Figure 1-7 as a model, enter the remaining field names, types, description, and sizes.

Field 2: Movie Title, Text, (none), 25

Field 3: Production Company, Text, (none), 20

Field 4: Category, Text, Use upper case (A, C, H, O, or S), 1

Date/Time Fields

The Release Date uses the Date/Time data type which is selected from the Data Type list box. When this option is selected, the size option disappears from the Field Properties area because the field size is determined by the date option you select. You will use the Format list box to select the short date format for this field.

■   Type **Release Date** as the fifth field name and press ENTER.

▶   *The text in the Data Type area is highlighted, and the arrow button is activated, as shown in Figure 1-7.*

Figure 1-8

- ■ Click on the arrow button.

  - ▶ *The Data Type list box opens.*

- ■ Select Date/Time format.

  - ▶ *Access closes the list box and removes the Size option from Field Properties.*

- ■ Move the pointer into the Field Properties Format area and click.

  - ▶ *A flashing cursor and an arrow button appear in the text area.*

- ■ Click on the arrow button and select Short Date.

  - ▶ *Short Date is added to the Format text box.*

We have just scratched the surface of possibilities when it comes to defining database records. The text boxes marked Validation Rule and Validation Text help database designers prompt the correct data entry and check for errors. Unfortunately, these topics and other validity checks must be left for another time.

SAVING THE TABLE DESIGN

Before continuing, you need to save the **table design** you just entered. The table design includes the field names, data types, data entry descriptions, and field formats.

- ■ From the File menu, select Save As.

  - ▶ *The Save As dialog box appears with Table 1 highlighted in the Table Name text box (see Figure 1-8).*

- ■ Type **MOVIES** and complete the command by clicking on OK or pressing ENTER.

  - ▶ *The table is added to the VIDSTORE database, and the table name is changed to Movies in the title bar.*

- ■ From the File menu, select Close.

  - ▶ *The display returns to the Access application window with the VIDSTORE database dialog box active.*

NOTE: If a table by the same name already exists, Access gives you the option of copying over the old table with the new or using a different name.

ENTERING DATA

The MOVIES table now exists as an empty shell on your disk. Your next step is to fill it with the names of the video tapes rented by Boomtown Video.

■ Make sure that MOVIES is highlighted in the VIDSTORE database dialog box.

■ Select Open.

▶ *A window with the empty MOVIES table is displayed.*

■ Maximize the MOVIES table window.

▶ *The MOVIES table fills the application window.*

Entering data into the table is basically the same as entering field names. After entering each field value, you press either the Tab or Enter keys to continue to the next entry. Access saves each record after all the fields are entered and checked for incompatibilities. As the insertion point moves from field to field the description (if any) you entered when setting up the MOVIES table appears in the status line. Furthermore, if incompatibilities are found, an error message appears in a special dialog box.

Should you discover that you neglected to enter one of the fields or made a mistake in a field definition or spelling of a field name, correcting the error is easy. From the <u>V</u>iew menu select Table <u>D</u>esign and correct the error. You can then continue entering data by using the <u>V</u>iew menu's Data<u>s</u>heet option.

■ Type **101** for the record 1 Movie ID and press ENTER.

▶ *The insertion point is moved to the record 1 Movie Title field.*

NOTE: When you make a mistake, use the Backspace key to back up and erase the problem. If the data has been entered, click the pointer when it is over the problem to move the insertion point. Then either use the Backspace or Delete keys to delete the entry. Remember Ctrl + Del and Ins will delete and insert records.

■ Type **Casablanca** for the record 1 Video Title and press ENTER.

▶ *The Production Company field is highlighted.*

■ Type **Warner Bros.** for the record 1 Production Company field and press ENTER.

▶ *The Category field is highlighted.*

■ Type **O** for Oldie in Category field and press ENTER.

▶ *The Release Date field is highlighted.*

■ Type **9/11/42** in the Release Date field and press ENTER.

▶ *After a pause to save the record, the record 2 Movie ID field is highlighted.*

P R A C T I C E   T I M E   1 - 2

Enter the following data into the MOVIES table. Do not be concerned if some titles are not fully displayed in the area provided. Arc in Raiders of the Lost Arc is purposely misspelled.

Record 2:	**102**	**African Queen**	**20th Century-Fox**	**O**	**10/12/51**
Record 3:	**103**	**Dirty Harry**	**Warner Bros.**	**A**	**3/18/71**
Record 4:	**104**	**Star Wars**	**20th Century-Fox**	**S**	**5/25/77**
Record 5:	**105**	**Friday the 13th**	**Paramount**	**H**	**1/9/80**
Record 6:	**106**	**Star Trek**	**Paramount**	**S**	**12/20/79**
Record 7:	**107**	**Raiders of the Lost Arc**	**Paramount**	**A**	**7/23/81**
Record 8:	**108**	**Ghostbusters**	**Columbia**	**C**	**7/16/84**
Record 9:	**109**	**Jaws**	**Universal**	**H**	**8/14/86**
Record 10:	**110**	**Platoon**	**Hemdale**	**A**	**12/5/86**
Record 11:	**111**	**The Godfather**	**Paramount**	**D**	**10/11/72**
Record 12:	**112**	**Die Hard**	**20th Century-Fox**	**A**	**6/30/88**

LOCATING RECORDS

The row/column format currently used to display the MOVIES table is called a ***datasheet.*** This format displays multiple records on the same screen and is one of several options you have for displaying data. A black triangle, the ***record selector***, in the far left column identifies the active record. In Figure 1-9, record 4 is the active record. The record number box above the status bar also identifies the active record as well as the current record count.

The contents of our MOVIES table are relatively small. However, you can imagine that a popular video rental store would have hundreds, if not thousands, of video tapes. As the table expands, you need ways of quickly finding records and moving around the table. The ***navigation buttons*** in Figure 1-9 let you move anywhere from the first to the last record in a table. These buttons also help you to move the record selector to the next or previous record. The navigation buttons are modeled after the forward and reverse buttons found on most tape players. The Record menu's Goto option provides the same alternatives (First, Last, Next, and Previous) along with a New record option.

■   Click on the First record navigation button, ⏮ .

Alternative: ALT+R, G then F.

Figure 1-9

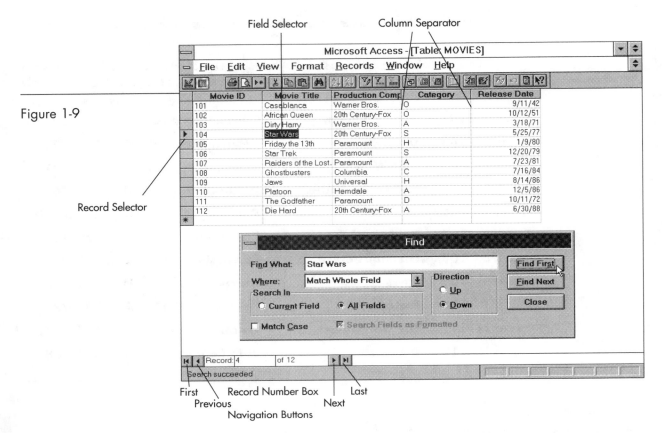

> The record selector moves to the first record (Casablanca).

■ Click on the Next record navigation button, ▶ .

Alternative: ALT+R, G then N.

> The record selector moves to record 2 (African Queen).

■ Click on the Last record navigation button, ▶| .

Alternative: ALT+R, G then L.

> The record selector moves to record 12 (Die Hard).

Access also lets you locate specific data, like a movie title or release date, by using the Edit menu's Find option. For instance, you could find information about the *Star Wars* movie using this method.

■ From the Edit menu, choose Find.

Alternative: Press CTRL+F or use the Find tool button, 🔍 .

> The Find dialog box opens.

■ Select the All Fields button.

■ Type **Star Wars** (don't forget space between words) into the Find What text box.

■ Select the Find First button.

▶ *Access highlights the Star Wars movie title; however, it may be hidden behind the dialog box.*

■ If necessary, drag the Find dialog box away from Movie ID 104 and the other Star Wars data as shown in Figure 1-9.

■ Select Close.

▶ *The Find dialog box closes, and the MOVIES table returns.*

P R A C T I C E   T I M E   1 - 3

Make record 12 the active record.

CHANGING COLUMN WIDTHS

On close examination of the datasheet, you will notice that the designated column widths are not wide enough to handle some data and field names. For example, the field name Production Company does not fit in the space provided. Neither does the movie title for record 7. While this will bother some people more than others, it is very simple to adjust the column widths. The line that falls between field names in the column headings is referred to as the **column separator.** When the pointer is moved over the column separator, it changes to a double arrow. At this time you can drag the column separator left or right to change the associated column width.

■ Move the pointer over the column separator between Production Company and Category.

▶ *The pointer changes to a double arrow.*

■ Drag the column separator to the right until the field name Production Company is completely visible.

P R A C T I C E   T I M E   1 - 4

1. Widen the Movie Title column until all of the title can be read.

2. Reduce the column width of the Movie ID and Category columns leaving enough space for the field names.

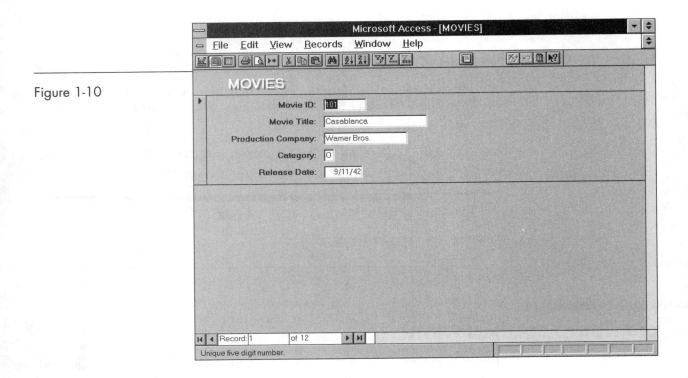

Figure 1-10

CREATING A FORM

While there are advantages in seeing several records at the same time when entering data using a datasheet, it can be cumbersome when long records are involved. In addition, business applications, like video rentals, often require special data entry screens that handle one record (rental) at a time. To meet these needs, Access offers users the option of displaying fields from a single record as a ***form.*** Figure 1-10 displays record 1 from the MOVIES table using the <u>V</u>iew menu's <u>F</u>orms option.

Wizards

The layout of a record when displayed as a form is completely flexible. You can customize the look, add your own labels, and change the field order used by the insertion point during data entry. However, an Access **Wizard** provides a fast and easy alternative. Wizards help users design database objects by automating common procedures. The AutoForm wizard will automatically create a professional-looking form for you at the click of a button. The form design in Figure 1-10 was created using the AutoForm wizard.

■   Click on the AutoForm tool button, 🔲.

   ▶   *After a pause, Access creates a data entry form for displaying MOVIES records.*

■   Maximize the form window.

   ▶   *Record 1 is displayed, as shown in Figure 1-10.*

■   Press PAGE DOWN.

   Alternative: Use Next button, ▶ .

   ▶   *The next record is displayed.*

The Page Down and Page Up keys are practical alternatives to the Previous and Next navigation button. In addition, pressing the Home key highlights the first field in the record while pressing the End key highlights the last field. These keyboard alternatives work in both a form view and a datasheet view.

PRACTICE TIME 1-5

Display record 8 in the MOVIES table.

Using a Data Entry Form

Data entry procedures using the form view are the same as those you used with the datasheet. After each entry press the Tab or Enter key to move to the next field. Any descriptive information about the field is displayed in the status line. To get to any empty screen for entering a new movie, you can either page down or use the Records menu's New option.

■   From the Records menu, choose Goto and select New.

   ▶   *An empty form is displayed, and the record number box indicates record 13 of 13.*

■   Enter the following data, pressing ENTER after each entry.

Movie ID: **113**

Movie Title: **Ghost**

Production Company: **Paramount**

Category: **D**

Release Date: **2/24/90**

   ▶   *A blank data entry form is displayed.*

P R A C T I C E   T I M E   1 - 6

Using the form view, enter the following records into the MOVIES table:

Record 14:	114	Pretty Woman	Touchstone	C	5/20/90
Record 15:	115	Dances with Wolves	Orion	A	11/9/90
Record 16:	116	Jurassic Park	Amblin	A	5/1/93
Record 17:	117	Adventures of *your name*	*your course name*	A	*Today's Date*

Records 18 & 19: Now enter your two favorite movies. Use Movie ID numbers 118 and 119. The category choices are as follows: A - Adventure, D - Drama, C - Comedy, H - Horror, O - Oldie (classics), and S - Science Fiction. Enter your best guess for release date and production company.

Saving the Form

Each database record is saved before the next record is entered. However, Access does not automatically save a new form. Before you continue, it would be best to store this form for future use. We will use Movies as the form name which also matches the table name.

■   From the File menu, select Close.

Alternative: Press CTRL+F4.

▶   *The Save As dialog box opens, asking if you wish to save changes to Form 'Form1'.*

■   Select Yes.

▶   *The Save As dialog box opens displaying default name Form1.*

■   Type **Movies** and complete the command.

▶   *The datasheet with the MOVIES table returns.*

NOTE: If the MOVIES table is not currently on the screen, open the Window menu and select the Table:MOVIES option.

On close examination of the datasheet you will notice that it does not contain records beyond number 12. Access does not automatically update a datasheet window when the table is updated using another window. The next time the datasheet opened, it will contain an updated view of the MOVIES table.

■   From the File menu, select Close.

▶   *Dialog box opens asking if you want to save changes to Table 'Movies'.*

■   Select Yes.

▶   *The display returns to the Access application window with the VIDSTORE database window active.*

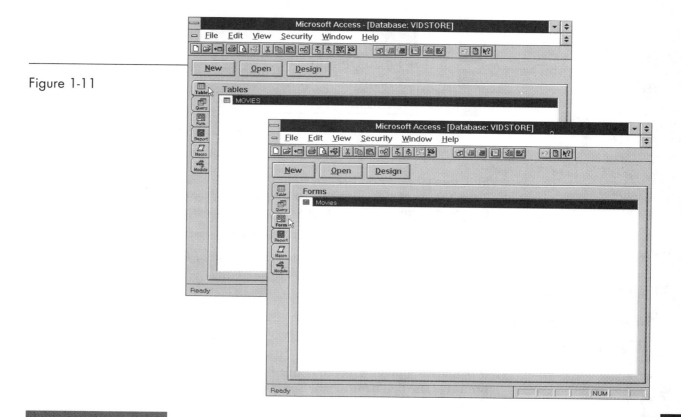

Figure 1-11

DATABASE OBJECTS AND VIEWS

The basic building block within an Access database is an ***object.*** You have already worked with two important objects: table and form. Other database objects, like query and report, are listed in the VIDSTORE database window currently on your screen. The sole purpose of these database objects is to organize data in a way that is easily accessible to you and others.

Currently, the VIDSTORE database contains two objects: the MOVIES table and the Movies form.

■ If necessary, select the Table button.

▶ *The window displays the MOVIES table, as shown at the top of Figure 1-11.*

■ Select the Form button.

▶ *The window lists the Movies form, as shown at the bottom of Figure 1-11.*

■ Click on the Open button.

▶ *The Movies form opens.*

The datasheet, form, and design views available to you are one way Access makes database data accessible. You will find that you can bounce

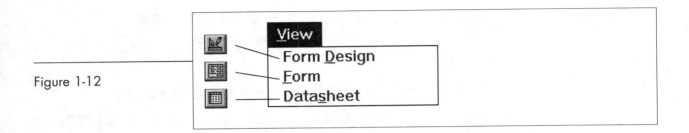

Figure 1-12

from one view to another depending on what you need to do with the data. From the form view currently on your screen, you can quickly change the view using the View menu options or tool buttons shown in Figure 1-12.

■   From the View menu, select Datasheet.

▶   *View changes to a row/column format showing all the MOVIES records you entered.*

PRINTING YOUR WORK

It is always a good habit to confirm the correct printer is selected prior to printing. The File menu Print Setup option enables you to make this check. If you have any question as to what the printer selection should be, check with your instructor.

■   From the File menu, select Print.

Alternative: Press CTRL+P or use the Print button, 🖨 .

▶   *The Print dialog box is displayed, as shown in Figure 1-13.*

Figure 1-13

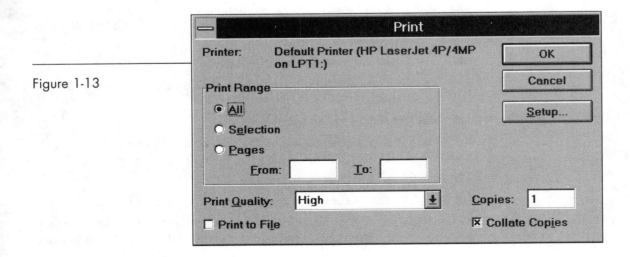

Take a close look at the dialog box on the screen. You will want to make sure you are printing one copy of all pages. These options should be the default settings.

■   Complete the command.

▶   *The printer displays a message box giving you a chance to cancel printing, then prints the table.*

CLOSING ACCESS WINDOWS

After the MOVIES table has been printed, you are done with this lesson and can close the table.

■   From the File menu, select Close.

▶   *The display returns to the VIDSTORE database window.*

EXITING ACCESS

It is a good habit to close all open windows before exiting Access. If you have made any recent changes to the database, Access will give you the option of saving these changes.

■   From the File menu, choose Close Database.

▶   *If recent changes have been made, Access gives you a chance to save changes, then returns to an empty Access application window.*

The procedure for exiting Access is similar to exiting any Windows-compatible software package. Selecting the Exit option from the File menu returns control back to Windows.

■   From the File menu, select Exit.

▶   *The program manager window is displayed.*

ENDING LESSON 1

Always end your Windows session from the Program Manager. This will guarantee you an opportunity to save any work you forgot to store on disk earlier. Before turning off your computer and the other associated hardware, ask your instructor about system shutdown procedures used at your school.

SUMMARY

❑   **Sophisticated database management systems (DBMS) integrate tables into relational databases.**

❑   **The Access DBMS works within the Windows operating environment and uses associated concepts and procedures.**

❑   **The Access application window offers a tool bar under the menu bar. The tool bar contains tool buttons representing common menu options.**

❑   **Access stores the user's database in the working directory. Each database is made up of objects which include tables and forms.**

❑   **Data records within a table are subdivided into fields. Each field is given a field name and designated as either text, memo, number, date/time, currency, counter, yes/no, or object-linking and embedding.**

❑   **When a field is designated as a primary key, it is required. Access will not add a new record to a table unless unique data is entered in the key field.**

❑   **Data is displayed in a row/column format as a datasheet or one record at a time in a form.**

❑   **Navigation buttons or the Edit menu's Find option are used to locate data within a table.**

❑   **Users can automatically create a data entry form using a wizard.**

❑   **Access uses Window's print manager to print data.**

❑   **As with all Windows compatible software, users quit Access by pulling down the File menu and selecting the Exit option.**

KEY TERMS

column separator	key	status bar
database management system (DBMS)	navigation buttons	table
	object	table design
datasheet	primary key	tool bar
field	record	tool button
field name	record selector	wizard
form	relational database	

COMMAND SUMMARY

File
New Database
Close Database
Save As
Print
Exit

Edit
Find

View
Table Design
Datasheet

Record
Goto

REVIEW QUESTIONS

1. How do fields, records, and tables form a relational database?

2. What steps do you follow to launch Access for Windows?

3. What is the function of the tool bar and the status bar?

4. Give an example of invalid data for each of the following field types: number, currency, date/time, and yes/no.

5. Why would having two records with the same primary key field value cause problems?

6. What information is included as part of the table design?

7. How do you save the table design?

8. How are navigation buttons used?

9. How do you change the column width in a datasheet?

10. What Access feature automatically creates a data entry form for users?

11. Identify three different Access views and explain how you change the view.

12. How do you print the contents of a datasheet?

13. How do you exit from Access?

EXERCISES

1. Create a database called PERSONAL.

a. Set up a new table called FRIENDS that will store information about people you know. Include in the table names, addresses, telephone number, birthday, and other information you would like to maintain about friends and relatives.

b. Create a data entry form.

c. Use data entry form to create five fictitious records. Use your name for record 1.

      d. Save the form as FRIENDS.

      e. Print the datasheet view of the FRIENDS table.

2. Create a new database called BUSINESS.

      a. Set up a new table called STOCKS that will serve as a personal stock portfolio manager. Include in the STOCKS table the following fields:

      Field 1 - Transaction Number (text, 6 characters, designate as primary key)

      Field 2 - Stock Name (text, 15 characters)

      Field 3 - Number of Shares (number)

      Field 4 - Purchase Price per Share (number)

      Field 5 - Date Purchased (date)

      Field 6 - Current Price per Share (number)

      b. Create a data entry form.

      c. Use the data entry form and financial page of your favorite newspaper to pick six stocks and enter related information into table. Transaction numbers should start at 1001 and increment by one, i.e., 1002, 1003, etc.

      d. Save the form as STOCKS.

      e. Print the datasheet view of the STOCKS table.

3. Create a table called SUPPLIER in the VIDSTORE database.

      a. Include the following fields in the table:

      Field 1 - Supplier Number (text, 6 characters, designate as primary key)

      Field 2 - Name (text, 25 characters)

      Field 3 - Street Address (text, 30 characters)

      Field 4 - City (text, 15 characters)

      Field 5 - State/Province (text, 2 characters)

      Field 6 - Zip/Postal Code (text, 10 characters)

      Field 7 - Telephone Number (text, 15 characters)

      Field 8 - Balance (number)

      b. Create a data entry form.

      c. Enter five records using a data entry form. Use your name for the first supplier and your imagination to fill in the remaining names, addresses, and other data.

      d. Save the form as SUPPLIER.

      e. Print the datasheet view of the SUPPLIER table.

2 Database Queries and Modifications

OBJECTIVES

Upon completing the material presented in this lesson, you should understand the following aspects of Access:

- ❑ **Using context-sensitive help**
- ❑ **Opening a database**
- ❑ **Updating (adding, deleting, or changing) data in a table**
- ❑ **Modifying a table's design**
- ❑ **Filtering data using query by example**
- ❑ **Sorting a dynaset**
- ❑ **Saving a query**
- ❑ **Printing a query dynaset**
- ❑ **Modifying a query**
- ❑ **Using comparison and logical operators in complex queries**

STARTING OFF

Database management systems, like Access 2.0 for Windows, allow you to access and organize vast amounts of data. If you know how to use this tool, significant increases in personal productivity can be achieved. All of this hinges on your ability to locate and access the databases holding information of use to you.

Turn on your computer and start the Windows program. Insert your data disk and then launch the Access program as you did in Lesson 1.

■ Turn on your computer.

■ Insert your data disk into the disk drive.

■ Launch Windows.

■ Open Access 2.0 group icon and Launch Access.

▶ *The Access application window is displayed.*

■ If necessary, maximize the application window.

When you start this lesson, you need access to the VIDSTORE database created in Lesson 1. The MOVIES table, shown in Figure 2-1, contains information customers like you could use when planning this weekend's video viewing.

When opening VIDSTORE you could encounter the **error message** shown in Figure 2-2. Error messages result when the computer system is unable to function properly or when you are about to do something you might regret. Well-written error messages provide explanations related to the problem or offer alternative courses of action.

Figure 2-1

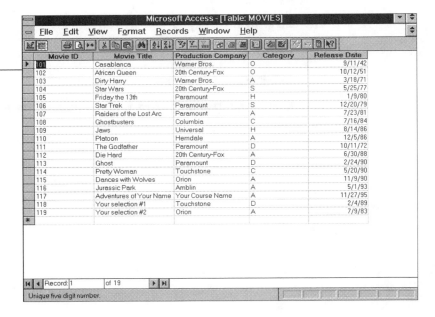

Movie ID	Movie Title	Production Company	Category	Release Date
101	Casablanca	Warner Bros.	O	9/11/42
102	African Queen	20th Century-Fox	O	10/12/51
103	Dirty Harry	Warner Bros.	A	3/18/71
104	Star Wars	20th Century-Fox	S	5/25/77
105	Friday the 13th	Paramount	H	1/9/80
106	Star Trek	Paramount	S	12/20/79
107	Raiders of the Lost Arc	Paramount	A	7/23/81
108	Ghostbusters	Columbia	C	7/16/84
109	Jaws	Universal	H	8/14/86
110	Platoon	Herndale	A	12/5/86
111	The Godfather	Paramount	D	10/11/72
112	Die Hard	20th Century-Fox	A	6/30/88
113	Ghost	Paramount	D	2/24/90
114	Pretty Woman	Touchstone	C	5/20/90
115	Dances with Wolves	Orion	A	11/9/90
116	Jurassic Park	Amblin	A	5/1/93
117	Adventures of Your Name	Your Course Name	A	11/27/95
118	Your selection #1	Touchstone	D	2/4/89
119	Your selection #2	Orion	A	7/9/83

Record: 1   of 19

Unique five digit number.

GETTING HELP

You encounter two different types of "problem" situations when working with software systems like Access. You initiate some situations by asking questions: "How do I do _____?" Other situations are forced upon you by the computer, as illustrated by the error message in Figure 2-2. This particular error message occurs when you attempt to access the database from a floppy disk drive that does not contain a formatted diskette or has its disk drive latch open.

Selecting the Retry button or pressing R clears the error message and the computer tries to read the diskette again. Selecting the Cancel button returns the display back to the Access application window. The most commonly used course of action is usually highlighted as the default button in the error message box. In Figure 2-2, the Retry button is the default option that you initiate by pressing the Enter key. You will also find the Access *User's Guide* a good reference source for additional information about error messages and other software features.

Situations where you ask "How do I do _____?" are handled by several Help features. These features include the Help menu and cue cards that walk you through different operations step-by-step. Both of these features provide ***context-sensitive help***. This means the information supplied by the help screens changes based on the Access feature currently being used.

Figure 2-2

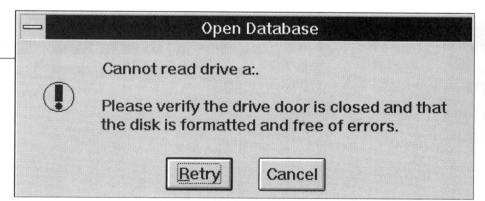

Cannot read drive a:.

Please verify the drive door is closed and that the disk is formatted and free of errors.

Retry   Cancel

NOTE: If any table is currently open, close it using the File menu's Close Database option.

■ Click on the Help menu.

Alternative: Press F1.

▶ *The help options are displayed.*

■ Select Contents.

▶ *A Help window with general information about Access appears, as shown at the top of Figure 2-3.*

The Help window contains a title bar and a row of help buttons above the workspace. The workspace contains information on a topic, here a short description of different Access features. The workspace can be scrolled. More information is available for any of the underlined topics called ***jump terms***. The top screen in Figure 2-3 contains the jump term <u>Using Microsoft Access</u>. A jump term or related icon is selected either by clicking on it using the mouse or by pressing Tab or Shift+Tab keys to highlight the topic and then pressing Enter. The Contents help button displays common concepts and jump terms. The <u>S</u>earch help button is used to locate a new jump term and related description.

- ■ Position the pointer over the <u>Using Microsoft Access</u> jump term.

  ▶ *The pointer changes to a pointing finger,* ⌐ *.*

- ■ Select the jump term.

  ▶ *The Using Microsoft Access window opens, as shown at the bottom of Figure 2-3.*

Control Box   Pointing Finger Pointer

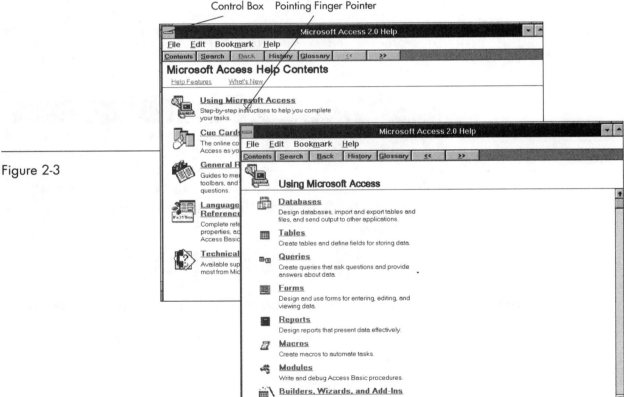

Figure 2-3

Since you need to open the VIDSTORE database, let's see what Help has to say about opening an existing database.

■ Click on the Databases jump term.

▶ *The Databases help window opens with a list of database-related jump terms.*

■ Select <u>Opening, Printing, Copying, Renaming, and Deleting</u> found at the bottom of the jump term list.

▶ *Opens a box with another list of jump terms.*

■ Choose Opening an Existing Database.

▶ *The Opening an Existing Database help window is displayed.*

■ After reading the help screen description, exit the Help window using the <u>F</u>ile menu.

Alternative: Double-click on the Help window control box.

▶ *The Help window is cleared from the Access application window.*

Another useful help feature is the Context-sensitive Help button. This feature helps you answer questions about icons and menu options found in the Access application window. Selecting this button and clicking on a menu option or toolbar button, automatically opens the related Help window.

■ Click on the Context-sensitive button, [?] .

▶ *Pointer changes to Context-sensitive pointer,* ? .

■ Open the <u>F</u>ile menu and use the Context-sensitive pointer to select <u>O</u>pen Database.

▶ *The Open Database Command (File Menu) window is displayed.*

■ After reading the help screen description, close the Help window.

▶ *The Help window is cleared from the Access application window.*

OPENING AN EXISTING DATABASE

The help screens you reviewed detailed the basic procedures for opening an existing database. Currently, at least two databases should be on your data disk: VIDSTORE and STUDENT as shown in Figure 2-4. Each database uses Access's default filename extension .MDB. The VIDSTORE database was created as part of the Lesson 1 tutorial and STUDENT is supplied to you by your instructor.

■   From the File menu, select Open Database.

Alternative: Use the Open Database button, ⬜ .

▶   *The Open Database dialog box is displayed.*

In figure 2-4, the Exclusive check box is checked. When this option is active like this, only one user at a time can access the database. That person would have to close the database before someone else could open it. The VIDSTORE database can be designated ***exclusive*** when working with it as a part of this lesson because there is no reason for more than one person to be using the data at the same time. In a real video store application, there could be reasons for turning this option off and having several clerks accessing movie titles and other data at the same time.

■   Verify that the disk drive and directory with your databases are shown in the Drives and Directories list boxes.

■   Click on VIDSTORE.MDB and finish the command by clicking on OK or pressing Enter.

Alternative: Double-click on VIDSTORE.MDB.

▶   *The database: VIDSTORE dialog box opens.*

■   With the Tables button active, select MOVIES, and click on Open.

▶   *The MOVIES table is displayed.*

Figure 2-4

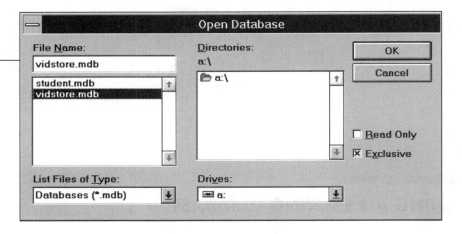

PRACTICE TIME 2-1

When necessary, complete the following actions. When you are done, your screen should look like Figure 2-1.

1. Display the MOVIES table as a datasheet.

2. Maximize the MOVIES window.

3. Widen the Movie Title column to fit the longest name.

4. Widen the Production Company column to fit the field name.

UPDATING A TABLE

Updating a table involves either adding, changing, or deleting records. In creating the MOVIES table in Lesson 1, you added 19 records to the empty table. Changing and deleting records is just as easy.

Changing a Field Entry

Making changes to field entry works just like the text editing feature of most word processing packages. Both the Delete (Del) and Backspace keys remove text. Delete removes text to the right of the flashing cursor (*insertion point*), while the Backspace key removes text to the left of the cursor. If a mistake is immediately caught the Edit menu's Undo Saved Record option or the Ctrl + Z keyboard alternative returns the changes back to the original format.

- Position the pointer to the right "c" in Raiders of the Lost Arc and click.
  - ▶ *A flashing cursor appears behind the "c" in "Arc."*
- Use the keyboard to backspace over "c" and then type **k**.
  - ▶ *Record 7's movie title now reads "Raiders of the Lost Ark."*
- Press the down arrow key.
  - ▶ *The cursor moves down to record 8's movie title after saving changes to record 7.*

Deleting a Record

The Delete key or Edit-Delete menu option removes highlighted records from a database table. The easiest way to highlight a record is to click on the record selector as shown in Figure 2-5. Because Access cannot undo

Figure 2-5

Record
Selector

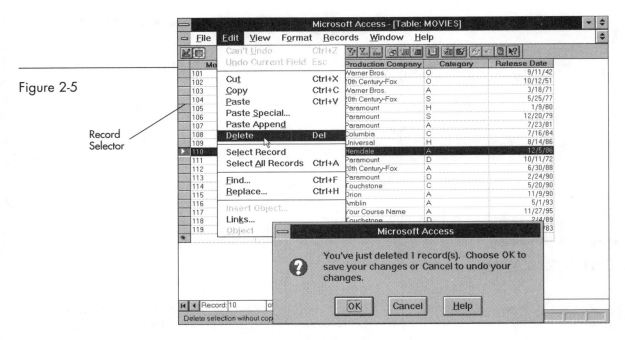

actions associated with removing a record, a warning box appears for you
to verify that the record is to be deleted.

■   Click on the record selector to the left of Movie ID 110.

▶   *Platoon record is highlighted, as shown in Figure 2-5.*

■   From the Edit menu, select Delete.

Alternative: Press Delete.

▶   *A Warning message asks you to OK the deletion of this
record.*

■   Complete the command by clicking on OK or pressing the
Enter key.

▶   *The record Platoon is removed from the table.*

PRACTICE TIME 2-2

Change the release date for *Jaws* to **4/20/75**.

MODIFYING A TABLE'S DESIGN

To allow for an expanded movie inventory, you need to increase the Movie
ID field to six characters and add a field called Ratings to the MOVIES

table. Ratings is a text field that stores the film industry rating of the movie (G, PG, PG13, and R for our purposes). Changes to a table's basic structure are made using the design view.

■ From the View menu, select Table Design.

Alternative: Use the Design button, 🖾 .

▶ *Display changes to design view similar to Figure 2-6.*

Expanding the Field Size

Making modifications to the Movie ID's field size is as simple as changing the 5 to a 6. However, great care is required when it comes to changing the design of a table because of the great potential for losing data. For example, changing the Movie ID field type from text to number would require the re-entry of related data. Expanding the ID field from three to four characters would not cause any problems. Making the ID field smaller would generate a warning message and potentially cause the loss of data that exceeded the new field size.

■ Select the Movie ID field name and change the 5 in the Field Size text box to a **6**.

■ Change the Movie ID Description to read "Unique **six** digit number".

Related error messages do not appear until you try to save the changes.

Figure 2-6

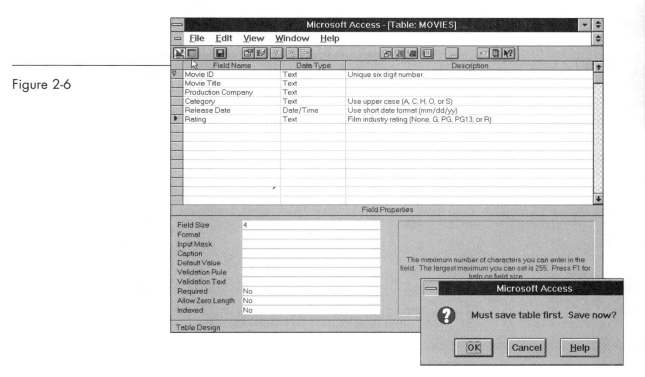

Adding a New Field

New fields are added to the table by inserting a new field name along with the related type, size, and description when appropriate.

- ■   Move the insertion point to the empty Field Name area under Release Date.

- ■   Type **Rating**.

  - ▶   *The new field name is added to the table design.*

- ■   Complete the field design with the following information:

    Data Type: **Text**

    Description: **Film industry rating (None, G, PG, PG13, or R)**

    Field Size: **4**

  - ▶   *The table design should look like Figure 2-6.*

- ■   From the <u>V</u>iew menu, choose Datasheet.

    Alternative: Use the Datasheet View button, 🖽 .

  - ▶   *A dialog box asking you to save table first is displayed as seen in Figure 2-6.*

- ■   Select OK.

  - ▶   *The new table design is stored, and you return to the datasheet view of the MOVIES table. Notice the empty Rating field next to Release Date.*

P R A C T I C E   T I M E   2 - 3

Update the MOVIES table with the following ratings. There are 18 ratings to add because *Platoon* was deleted.

ID	RATING	ID	RATING
101	**None**	111	**R**
102	**None**	112	**R**
103	**R**	113	**PG13**
104	**PG**	114	**R**
105	**R**	115	**PG13**
106	**G**	116	**PG13**
107	**G**	117	**PG**
108	**PG**	118	*your choice*
109	**R**	119	*your choice*

CREATING A QUERY

What is the point of having information if you can't use it? Every DBMS has some means of answering user queries about data. A **query** is a question you ask concerning database data which is in a format that prompts Access to display selected data. The selected data is called a **dynaset**, which looks like a table, but is really a special view of data from one or more tables. A video store customer might ask for a list of all the movies classified as adventure. The dynaset set would be the movie titles of all the adventure movies. Someone else could ask for the list of adventure movies in order from oldest to newest or for a printed copy of the list.

■   From the File menu, choose New, and then select Query.

   Alternative: Use the New Query button, 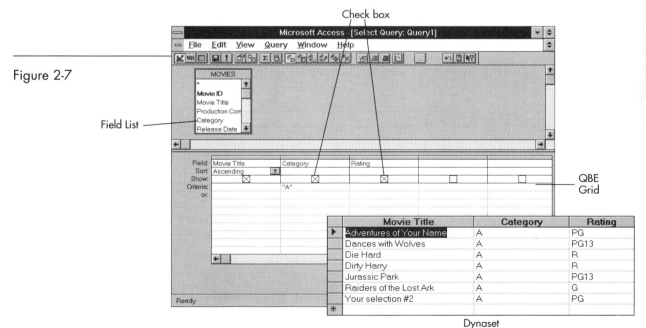.

   ▶   *Opens New Query dialog box.*

■   Select New Query.

   ▶   *The Select Query window is displayed.*

The top screen in Figure 2-7 illustrates a **select query**. The field names Movie Title, Category, and Rating are in the QBE (Query-By-Example) grid that makes up the bottom half of the query window. When an X appears in the check box under each field name, Access adds related data to the dynaset, also shown in Figure 2-7. If a check mark does not appear in the Show area, the related field can be used as a basis for selecting data, but is not included in the dynaset.

Figure 2-7

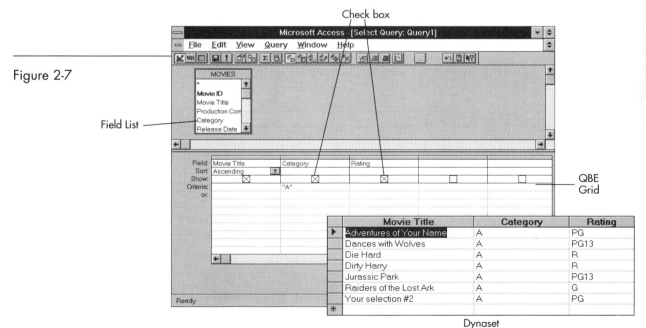

Dynaset

As you can see, the select query gets its name because it allows the user to selectively display database data. A select query is one of the most common types of queries. Other types will be discussed later. Building queries is fun and represents the true power of a DBMS.

To select all movie titles:

■ Move the pointer into the first Field area of the QBE grid and click.

  ▶ *An insertion point and a down arrow appear in the Field area.*

■ Click on the down arrow.

  ▶ *The list box that displays field names from the MOVIES table opens, as shown in Figure 2-8.*

■ Select Movie Title.

  ▶ *The field name is added to the first Field area ,and an X is placed in the Show check box.*

■ From the Query menu, select Run.

  Alternative: Press the Run button, 🔲 .

  ▶ *A dynaset is displayed with all 18 movie titles.*

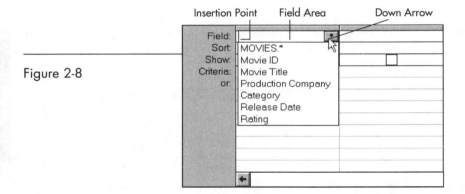

Figure 2-8

Query Design Window

The query results, the dynaset, are displayed as a datasheet. Some people like to think that a query works like a filter, displaying only the data selected from one or more tables. The QBE grid found in the query design view identifies the selection criterion used by the query. The View-Query Design command or Design View button returns the display to the design view.

■ From the View menu, select Query Design.

  Alternative: Use the Design View button, 🔲 .

  ▶ *The Select Query window is displayed.*

Selection Criteria

Field names can also be added to the QBE grid by dragging the name from the field list down into the Field area of the grid. To demonstrate this *drag-and-drop* alternative, you will drag the Category field name into the QBE grid and use it to identify all the adventure movies in the MOVIES table. On closer inspection of Figure 2-7, you will see the ***expression*** *"A"* below the Category check mark in the Criteria area. It specifies that only movies where the *category* = *"A"* are listed. An expression identifies the criteria Access uses to add data to the dynaset. Where an exact match, like uppercase A, is needed, enclose the character(s) in double quotes.

To select all the adventure movies:

■ Click on the field name Category in the MOVIES list box and drag it into the field area to the right of Movie Title.

▶ *Category is added to the QBE grid (similar to Figure 2-7).*

■ Click the pointer under the Category check box in the Criteria area.

▶ *The insertion point is activated.*

■ Type **"A"**.

▶ *Adds expression to Criteria area.*

■ Run the query by clicking on the Run button, ▣.

▶ *A new Dynaset window appears with at least six adventure movie titles. The number of adventure movies could exceed six if you added movies in this category.*

Sorting the Dynaset

In addition, movie titles can be displayed in alphabetical order from A to Z by designating the Sort area under movie title as ascending. Your other options are descending order (Z-A) or not sorted. When sorting number fields, ascending order is from smallest number to the largest, while descending order is from the largest number to the smallest.

To sort adventure movies by Movie Title:

■ Return to the query design view by clicking on the Design button, ▣.

■ Click the pointer under Movie Title in the Sort area.

▶ *The insertion point is activated, and a down arrow is displayed.*

■ Click on the down arrow.

▶ *The list box that displays sorting options opens.*

■ Select Ascending.

■   Run the query.

▶   *The dynaset includes adventure movies in alphabetical order.*

PRACTICE TIME 2-4

Use Figure 2-7 as a model for the final results.

1.   Add the Rating field to the QBE grid and then run the query.

2.   Use the column separator to widen the Movie Title column to fit the longest name in the dynaset.

Saving a Query

Saving regularly used queries will improve your productivity because you can quickly answer commonly asked What-if questions by opening the query and running it again. If the table has been recently updated, the new dynaset reflects these changes.

You save a new query by using the File-Save As command. Otherwise, Access will ask you if you want to save the query when you close it. In either case, you will be given a chance to change the default query name, Query1, to a more descriptive name. The query name can be up to 64 characters, and spaces are acceptable. If you use the File-Save command or Save button at this time, Access still asks if you want to change the default query name.

■   From the File menu, select Save Query As.

Alternative: Use the Save button, 🖫 .

▶   *The Save As dialog box opens.*

■   Type **Adventure Movies** and complete the command.

▶   *The Select Query window returns with the new query name in the title bar.*

Before printing, you will turn off the gridlines.

Turning Off Gridlines

While gridlines help the eye track field entries across the screen, some people like to use Format-Gridlines to turn them off when printing. A check mark appears in front of the Gridlines menu option when the lines are on as shown in Figure 2-9. Selecting the same menu option again turns it off.

■   From the Format menu, select Gridlines.

▶   *The check mark is removed from the menu, and the lines are removed from the display.*

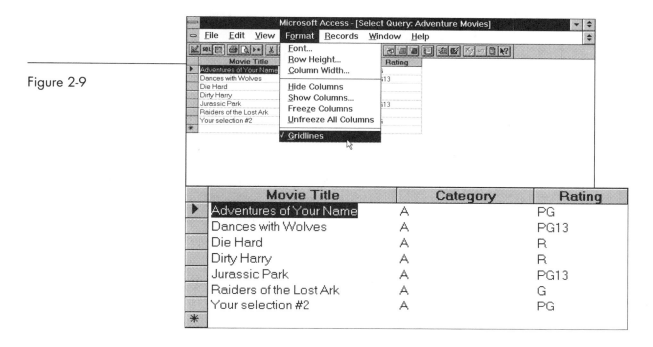

Figure 2-9

Printing a Dynaset

Access's File-Print command creates a printed report from data in any active window.

■   Check to make sure the printer is on and ready to print.

■   Click on the Print button, 🖨.

▶   *The Print dialog box is displayed.*

■   Make sure you are printing one copy and complete the command.

▶   *One copy of the dynaset is printed, with the query name Adventure Movies at the top.*

PRACTICE TIME 2-5

1. Turn on the gridlines.

2. Return to the query design view.

Removing Fields from a Query

Fields are not transferred to the query dynaset when the X is removed from the Show area in the QBE grid. However, queries can still be based on field values even when the field itself is not included in the dynaset. For example, if the X in the Category check box is removed, but the expression "A" remains, the query is still limited to adventure movies.

- From the query design view, click on the X in the Category Show area.

    ▶ *The X is removed from the box, but the expression "A" remains in the Criteria area.*

- Run the query.

    ▶ *The dynaset contains adventure movie titles and the movies' ratings.*

Fields are removed from the QBE grid by highlighting the field name and pressing the Delete key or, one character at a time, by using the Delete or Backspace keys. Related search criteria, sorting order, and other information in the QBE grid are not removed until the insertion point is moved to another field by pressing one of the arrows keys or Enter.

- Return to the query design view.

- Click to the left of the Category field name in the QBE grid.

    ▶ *An insertion point appears in front of the field name.*

- Use the BACKSPACE or the DELETE key to remove the field name, then press LEFT ARROW.

    ▶ *The expression "A" is removed from the QBE grid, and the insertion point moves to the next field.*

PRACTICE TIME 2-6

Create a query that identifies all the movie titles and related ratings for movies produced by Paramount. The dynaset should include the Movie Title and Rating fields, but not Production Company. Use **Paramount Movies** as the query name and print the dynaset.

COMPLEX QUERIES

Quite often, the selection criteria used within a query will involve data from several fields or different field values from the same field. These **complex queries** use multiple criteria along with two **logical operators**: *AND* and *OR*. For example, a complex query could search for information from two separate fields, such as adventure movies with a PG13 rating. In this case the Category field must equal A *and* the Rating field value must equal

PG13. Other times, complex queries search for different values within the same field, such as a customer who wants a list of either adventure or drama movies. In this situation the category field equals A *or* D.

Using the OR Operator

When using the OR operator, only one of the criteria needs to exist for the data to be included in the dynaset. In Figure 2-10, either adventure movies or dramas meet the selection criteria. In this situation no movie would fall into both categories so the OR operator has to be used.

To get a list of all the adventure movies or dramas:

- ■ Display the query design view.

  - ▶ *The Movie Title and the Rating fields in the QBE grid should already be marked for inclusion in the dynaset.*

- ■ Remove any other field names from the QBE grid.

- ■ Add the Category field name to the QBE grid.

  - ▶ *Three fields should appear in the QBE grid: Movie Title, Rating, and Category.*

- ■ In the Criteria area under the Category field, type **"A" Or "D"**.

  - ▶ *The Select Query window should look like Figure 2-10.*

NOTE: Access changes the *o* in *or* to an uppercase *O*.

- ■ Run the query.

  - ▶ *You get a list with at least eight records including one with your name.*

Figure 2-10

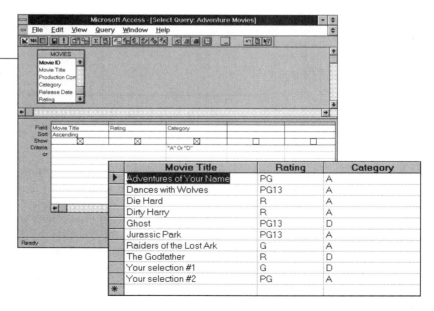

When different fields are used, the second condition is placed in the "or" area found below the Criteria area. Consider a situation where you are looking for movies with a G rating *or* adventure movies. For this query to work, "A" is placed in the Criteria area below Category, while "G" is placed in the or area below Rating.

Access defaults to using the AND operator when more than one Criteria area is filled-in. A query with "A" and "G" in their respective Criteria areas would produce a dynaset listing G rated adventure movies.

Using the AND Operator

When the AND operator is used, every selection criteria must be met before the data is added to the dynaset. In the next query you are to develop, a movie must be rated PG13 as well as have a Category field equal to A.

To select all adventure movies with a rating of PG13:

- ■   Return to the query design view.

- ■   Remove **Or "D"** from the Category Criteria area.

- ■   Type **"PG13"** in the Rating Criteria field.

    ▶   *The QBE grid should look like Figure 2-11.*

- ■   Run the query.

    ▶   *You get a dynaset which includes at least 2 records: Dances with Wolves and Jurassic Park.*

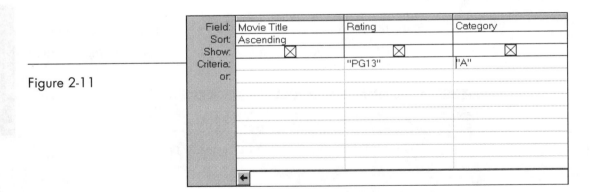

Figure 2-11

Using Wildcard Characters

In some situations, you need to give Access flexibility in determining which fields are included in the dynaset. For example, some video store customers might find either PG or PG13 movies acceptable. You could use the OR operator to define the selection criteria as *"PG" Or "PG13"*. An interesting alternative is to use the expression *Like "PG*"*. The asterisk (*) is a **wildcard character.** This means that any combination of characters are acceptable where the * is located in the expression. In this case, the rating meets the selection criteria if it starts with PG.

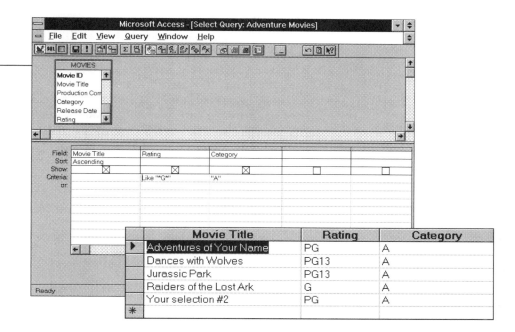

Figure 2-12

To select all the adventure movies with some type of PG rating:

■   Return to the query design view.

■   Replace the expression "PG13" with **Like "PG*"**.

■   Run the query.

▶   *You get a list that includes the movies with your name.*

Wildcard characters can precede or follow selected characters in the selection criteria. Movies with a PG, PG13, or G rating all contain the letter G in the rating. Modifying the Ratings Criteria area to *Like "*G*"* would cover any movie except those with an R rating.

■   Return to the query design view.

■   Replace the Rating Criteria Like "PG*" with **Like "*G*"**.

▶   *The QBE grid should look like the top of Figure 2-12.*

■   Run the query.

▶   *You get a dynaset that includes all adventure movies with a G, PG, or PG13 rating, as shown in Figure 2-12.*

Using Comparison Operators

Data ranges can be identified as part of the selection criteria by using the following ***comparison operators***:

<	less than
<=	less than or equal to

> greater than

>= greater than or equal to

These operators work with text, dates, numbers, and other types of data. For instance, movies released before 1980 are identified by the expression <1/1/80 as shown in Figure 2-13. An expression can contain several comparison and logical operators. If you added a field that identified how many minutes each movie ran, you could use the expression >60 And <120 to identify movies running over 60 minutes but under 120 minutes.

You should always double-check the logic behind complex queries. It is easy to create a query that does not produce the expected results because the operators are used incorrectly within the selection criteria. Consider again the example above that used movie run times. If the expression used OR instead of AND, then the expression >60 Or <120 would not eliminate any movies from the dynaset.

Movies released before 1980:

■   Return to the query design view.

■   Remove **Like "*G*"** and **"A"** from the Criteria areas.

■   Add Release Date to the QBE grid.

■   Make **<1/1/80** the Release Date criteria.

  ▶   *The QBE grid should look like the top of Figure 2-13.*

■   Run the query.

  ▶   *You get a dynaset that includes all movies released before 1980, as shown in Figure 2-13.*

NOTE: Access adds the # symbol to the beginning and end of the date when it recognizes the entry as a date.

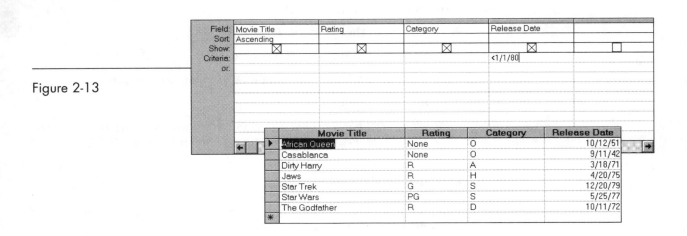

Figure 2-13

P R A C T I C E   T I M E   2 - 7

1. Print a dynaset with the movie titles and the release dates of all movies released before 1980 in ascending order by release date. Save the query using the query name **Released Before 1980**.

2. Print a list of all the horror movies by title and rating. Do NOT include the Category field in the dynaset and save the query using the name **Horror Movies**.

3. Print a list with the movie title, rating, and category of any movie with the word "Ghost" in the title or in the horror category. Save the query using the name **Ghost Movies**.

4. Close all open query windows.

5. Return to the VIDSTORE database dialog box and maximize the window if necessary.

6. Displays the Query list as shown in Figure 2-14.

DELETING QUERY FROM DATABASE

New queries are developed when they help answer often-asked questions. In these situations the query can be saved and opened again whenever it is needed. Having the query saved on disk is better than using a printed copy of the results because the most up-to-date data is used every time the query is opened and run.

However, every computer user must do a little "housekeeping" once in a while and delete from disk queries, forms, and other database objects that are not being used. Because Access objects are interlinked in many applications, great care must be taken when deleting any object. You could delete a query that is used as a basis for a report, making the report useless.

You are going to delete the Ghost Movies query you created as part of the last Practice Time. The procedure is straightforward. You simply highlight the object name in the database dialog box and press the Delete key. The object is deleted once you confirm that the correct object has been selected.

■   Select Ghost Movies in the Queries list box.

▶   *The query name is highlighted, as shown in Figure 2-14.*

■   Press DELETE.

▶   *The confirmation dialog box opens, also shown in Figure 2-14.*

Figure 2-14

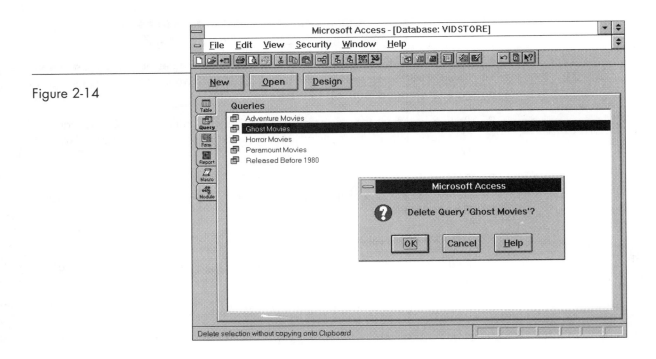

■ Confirm the deletion by clicking on OK or pressing ENTER.

▶ *Ghost Movies is removed from the query list.*

ENDING LESSON 2

This is the end of Lesson 2. Close all open windows and exit Access. If you are done with the computer, follow the recommended procedures for shutting down the computer system.

■ Close all open Access windows.

■ Exit Access.

SUMMARY

❑ **Error messages occur when the computer cannot perform a task or the user is about to get into trouble.**

❑ **Context-sensitive help answers your questions about specific software features. The *User's Guide* also explains software features and error messages.**

❏ **Updating a table involves adding, changing, or removing records.**

❏ **Access organizes records in a table by the key field, also known as the primary key. Tables without a primary key organize records in data entry order.**

❏ **Take special precautions when modifying a table's design. Some changes result in the loss of data.**

❏ **You can extract and sort information from a table using a query. Access uses a query-by-example (QBE) format within the query design view.**

❏ **A query's QBE grid can include expressions that filter the data going into the dynaset.**

❏ **Dynasets can be printed just like data from a table.**

❏ **Data in a dynaset can be sorted into another order.**

❏ **Any object can be removed from the database by highlighting its name in the database dialog box and pressing the Delete key.**

KEY TERMS

comparison operators
complex queries
context-sensitive help
dynaset
error message

exclusive
expression
jump term
logical operators
query

select query
updating
wildcard character

DATABASE

COMMAND SUMMARY

File
New ▶ Query
Open Database

Edit
Undo Saved Record
Delete

View
Query Design

Format
Gridlines

Query
Run

Help
Contents

REVIEW QUESTIONS

1. What are two resources, not counting the instructor, you could use to help solve problems that arise when using Access?

2. How do you access data from an existing database?

3. What procedures are used to change existing data in a table or to delete a record?

4. Identify two situations in which data would be lost when modifying a table's structure.

5. How is a dynaset created?

6. What are two ways to add a field to the dynaset?

7. How is data sorted in a dynaset?

8. How do you remove gridlines from a table or dynaset?

9. Explain how you can use a field value as part of a query's selection criteria without including the value within the dynaset.

10. What is the difference between using the OR operator in a complex query and using the AND operator?

11. Explain how a wildcard character is used in an Access QBE grid selection criteria.

12. Identify four different comparison operators.

13. How do you delete a query from the database?

EXERCISES

1. Update the FRIENDS table in the PERSONAL database and set up queries.

    a. Add four new records that reflect the following data:
        - Two male names with birth dates in April and September.
        - Two female names with birth dates in September and December.

    b. Change the addresses and phone numbers of any two of the original five entries.

    c. Delete one of the original five records, but do not delete your record.

    d. Create queries that look for the following information. Print each dynaset as a datasheet and save each query. Include in each dynaset all the fields used by the FRIENDS table. Hint: More than one wildcard character can be used and Access makes a distinction between 09 and 9 when used in a date.
        - All September birth dates.
        - All September or December birth dates.

  e. Print the FRIENDS table.

2. Update the STOCKS table in the BUSINESS database and set up queries.

  a. Modify the table design by changing the Purchase Price per Share and Current Price per Share fields to a currency data type.

  b. Update the Current Price per Share in each record to reflect the most current closing share price.

  c. Add four new stocks to the portfolio. Incorporate the following data into these records:

Transaction #	# of Shares	Purchase Price	Current Price
1007	**100**	**$18.27**	**$21.00**
1008	**400**	**$10.15**	**$11.75**
1009	**700**	**$7.36**	**$6.50**
1010	**200**	**$14.95**	**$12.00**

  d. Increase by 100 shares the number of shares you own for transactions 1002 and 1005.

  e. Delete transaction 1003.

  f. Create queries that look for the following information. Print each dynaset as a datasheet and save each query. Include in each dynaset all six fields found in the STOCKS table.

   - All holdings of more than 300 shares.

   - All holdings of more than 300 shares where the current price is higher than $10.

3. Update the RENTALS and INV table in the STUDENT database and set up queries.

  a. Add four new rentals to the RENTALS table and include the following data:

Customer No.	Tape No.	Date Out	Date In
941111	**42138**	**09/16/94**	**09/17/94**
941111	**47739**	**09/21/94**	**09/22/94**
941111	**50616**	**10/05/94**	**10/07/94**
941111	**48419**	**10/11/94**	**10/12/94**

  b. Movies with tape numbers 48420 and 50617 have been returned damaged. Change their available status in the INV table to an uppercase **N**.

  c. Tape number 48929 is damaged beyond repair and should be deleted from the INV table.

  d. Using the INV table, create queries that look for the following information. Print each dynaset as a datasheet and save each query. Include in each dynaset all five fields found in the INV table.

   - All movies with a purchase price over $35.

   - The movies with a purchase price over $35 that were purchased before 1990.

3 Creating Reports and Two Table Queries

OBJECTIVES

Upon completing the material presented in this lesson, you should understand the following aspects of Access 2.0:

- ❏ **Attaching a database to other tables**
- ❏ **Using the Mailing Label wizard**
- ❏ **Understanding report design terminology**
- ❏ **Using the Groups/Totals wizard**
- ❏ **Creating a two-table query**
- ❏ **Reassigning a report to a new query or table**
- ❏ **Customizing headings**
- ❏ **Printing reports**

STARTING OFF

Turn on your computer, start Windows, and then launch the Access 2.0 for Windows program as you did in previous lessons. Insert your data disk and set the working directory if necessary. Maximize the Access application window.

■ Insert your data disk into the disk drive.

■ Launch Access.

▶ *The Access application window is displayed.*

■ Open the VIDSTORE database.

■ If necessary, maximize the application window.

ATTACHING OTHER DATABASE TABLES

It is time to link the VIDSTORE database to the customer, inventory (inv), and rentals tables found in the STUDENT database supplied by your instructor. Access provides two ways of incorporating files used by other database management software, including other Access files. When you *import* a file, it is converted into an Access format. *Attaching* to another database table leaves the data in its original format, while allowing you to display and update it. However, you cannot change the design of any objects in the attached database.

The three tables, CUSTOMER, INV, and RENTALS, are all in a native Access format and do not need to be imported. You will attach the VIDSTORE database to each of these tables. Together with the MOVIES table (see Figure 3-1), they represent an integrated relational database system.

■ From the File menu, select Attach Table.

▶ *The Attach dialog box opens, as shown at the top of Figure 3-2.*

■ Verify that the data source is Microsoft Access and complete the command by clicking on OK or pressing Enter.

▶ *The Select Microsoft Access Database dialog box opens.*

The dialog box on your screen is essentially the same as the Open dialog box. You identify the drive, directory, and database name of the data you want to attach. The Exclusive check box is also found in the Open dialog box. When this option is active, only one user can access the database. That person would have to close it before someone else could open it. Since you could be sharing these tables with other students on a network, you should make sure the Exclusive option is NOT active.

Figure 3-1

CUSTOMER TABLE

Customer Number	First Name	Last Name	Address	City	State/Prov	Zip/Postal Code
881464	Alice	Harris	734 Mercury Drive	Hackley	MI	49442
882882	John	Wilson	12456 East Stone R	Grand Lake	MI	49457
884317	George	Miller	789 Robins Road	Wilson Park	MI	49480
886951	Sandy	Davis	4533 Ritter Drive	Hackley	MI	49442
891254	Todd	Evans	1351 Willow Lane	Hackley	MI	49441
894239	Mary	Richardson	1728 Apple Avenue	Grand Lake	MI	49457
896444	Frank	Stevens	96381 Pinewood	Hackley	MI	49442
897062	Charles	Billings	1879 Strong	Wilson Park	MI	49480
898837	Carol	Taylor	8845 Garfield Road	Grand Lake	MI	49457
899111	Roxanne	Little	3657 Wilson	Hackley	MI	49442
913271	Bill	Alberts	682 Williams	Wilson Park	MI	49480
915968	Martha	Young	226 E. 120th	Hackley	MI	49443
916389	Judy	Harris	3226 Wolf Lake Ro	Hackley	MI	49441
917222	Alan	McCarthy	17984 Cove Harbor	Hackley	MI	49441
919977	Dan	Kamp	456 State	Hackley	MI	49443

RENTALS TABLE

Customer Number	Tape Number	Date Out	Date In
881464	16828	8/8/92	8/9/92
881464	44332	8/19/92	8/20/92
881464	47739	8/30/92	
881464	48419	8/9/92	8/10/92
881464	48800	8/12/92	8/13/92
881464	50613	8/5/92	6/6/92
882882	40013	8/22/92	8/23/92
882882	46599	8/16/92	8/17/92
882882	48422	8/18/92	8/19/92
882882	48799	8/3/92	8/4/92
882882	48801	8/21/92	
882882	63456	8/11/92	8/12/92
884239	47315	8/24/92	8/25/92
884317	16828	8/15/92	8/17/92
884317	37612	8/8/92	8/9/92
884317			
884317			
884317			
884317			
886951			
886951			

INVENTORY TABLE

Tape Number	Movie ID	Available	Purchase Date	Purchase Price
16827	101	Y	1/5/93	$39.75
16828	101	Y	1/5/93	$39.75
23184	113	Y	3/5/93	$42.85
23185	113	Y	3/5/93	$42.85
23186	113	Y	3/5/93	$42.85
23187	113	Y	10/5/93	$42.85
37611	114	N	3/17/93	$35.60
37612	114	Y	3/17/93	$35.60
39955	111	Y	4/2/93	$29.95
39956	111	Y	4/2/93	$29.95
40012	102	Y	3/27/88	$39.75
40013	102	Y	3/27/88	$39.75
40014	102	Y	3/27/88	$39.75
42137	109	Y	7/9/93	$35.60
42138	109	Y	7/9/93	$35.60
42139				
43765				
43766				
44331				
44332				
46130				
46131				
46599				
47314				
47315				

MOVIES TABLE

Movie ID	Movie Title	Production Company	Category	Release Date	Rating
101	Casablanca	Warner Bros.	O	9/11/42	None
102	African Queen	20th Century-Fox	O	10/12/51	None
103	Dirty Harry	Warner Bros.	A	3/18/71	R
104	Star Wars	20th Century-Fox	S	5/25/77	PG
105	Friday the 13th	Paramount	H	1/9/80	R
106	Star Trek	Paramount	S	12/20/79	G
107	Raiders of the Lost Ark	Paramount	A	7/23/81	G
108	Ghostbusters	Columbia	C	7/16/84	PG
109	Jaws	Universal	H	4/20/75	R
111	The Godfather	Paramount	D	10/11/72	R
112	Die Hard	20th Century-Fox	A	6/30/88	R
113	Ghost	Paramount	D	2/24/90	PG13
114	Pretty Woman	Touchstone	C	5/20/90	R
115	Dances with Wolves	Orion	A	11/9/90	PG13
116	Jurassic Park	Amblin	A	5/1/93	PG13
117	Adventures of Your Name	Your Course Name	A	11/27/95	PG
118	Your selection #1	Touchstone	D	2/4/89	G
119	Your selection #2	Orion	A	7/9/83	PG

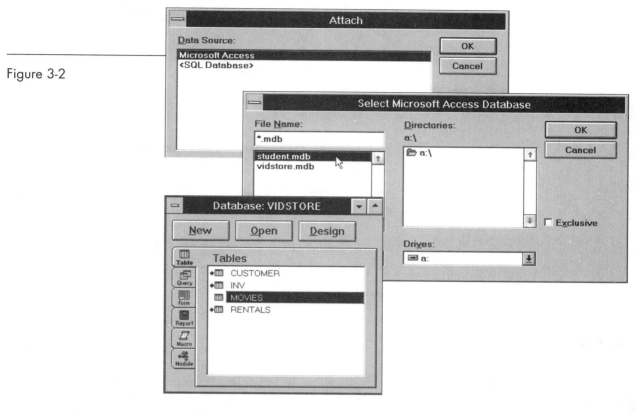

Figure 3-2

- Verify the Exclusive check box is empty.

- Select **student.mdb** and complete the command.

  ▶ *The Attach Tables dialog box opens, as shown at the bottom of Figure 3-2.*

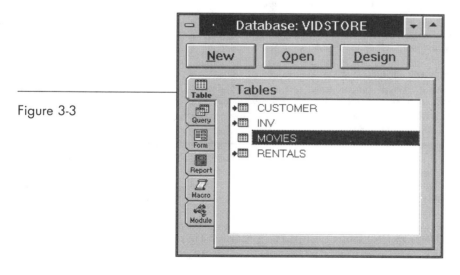

Figure 3-3

DATABASE

■ Choose the CUSTOMER table and complete the command.

▶ *After a pause, a confirmation box confirms that the table was successfully attached. Do not continue until you have successfully attached the table.*

■ Select OK.

▶ *The display returns to the Attach Tables dialog box.*

P R A C T I C E   T I M E   3 - 1

1. Attach the INV and RENTALS tables to the VIDSTORE database.

2. Close the Attach Tables dialog box.

The VIDSTORE Database dialog box should look like Figure 3-3.

CREATING REPORTS

The queries used in earlier lessons were practical demonstrations of how users can access database tables in ways that meet their personal needs. The need for concise, up-to-date, and easy-to-read information is behind the development of many relational databases. Reports represent another Access feature that allows you to customize data presentations. A report is designed to be printed on paper and used away from the database and computer system that created it. This lesson focuses on the design and development of printed reports using tables or queries.

P R A C T I C E   T I M E   3 - 2

1. Open the CUSTOMER table.

2. Maximize the CUSTOMER window, if necessary.

3. Add your name and address to the CUSTOMER table. Your customer number is 941111, and your rental status is U (unrestricted).

MAILING LABELS

The CUSTOMER table contains customer names, addresses, telephone numbers, and rental status. Rental status is either U (unrestricted) or R (restricted). You will use Access's report wizard to create mailing labels for fliers being sent to all customers.

New Report Wizard

Mailing labels are just one of several report formats that can be automatically generated by an Access wizard. The Report Wizard is used to quickly create professional looking documents. Quite often, the wizard report design is then customized. Figure 3-4 illustrates samples of the different report formats that are available through the New Report wizard. The last option shown in Figure 3-4, the AutoReport wizard, has its own button in the tool bar (🖺) and produces a Single-Column report without additional questions to the user.

■ From the File menu, choose New, then select Report.

  Alternative: Use the New Report button, 🖺.

  ▶ *The New Report dialog box is displayed with CUSTOMER highlighted in the Select a Table/Query text box.*

■ Select the Report Wizards button.

  ▶ *The Report Wizards list box opens; it is similar to the one in Figure 3-4.*

■ Choose the Mailing Label wizard and complete the command.

  ▶ *After a pause, Access displays the Mailing Label Wizard dialog box.*

You will use this wizard to create mailing labels that use fields from the CUSTOMER table. Spaces, commas, and other common punctuation found on mailing labels are added to the design by selecting the appropriate button. Pressing the associated key on the keyboard *does not* work and can have unexpected results. The mailing label design in Figure 3-5 produced the mailing labels shown in Figure 3-4. You will use the same design.

■ Select **First Name** in the Available fields list box.

  ▶ *The field name is highlighted.*

■ Click on the single right arrow button, ▷.

  ▶ *The First Name moves to Label appearance area.*

NOTE: Clicking on the left arrow button (◁) would move unwanted fields or punctuation marks out of the appearance area.

■ Click on the Space button to add a space after the first name field.

  ▶ *A small dot is placed after the First Name in the Label appearance area, as shown in Figure 3-5.*

Figure 3-4

Group statistic based on a number field

Each field gets a line

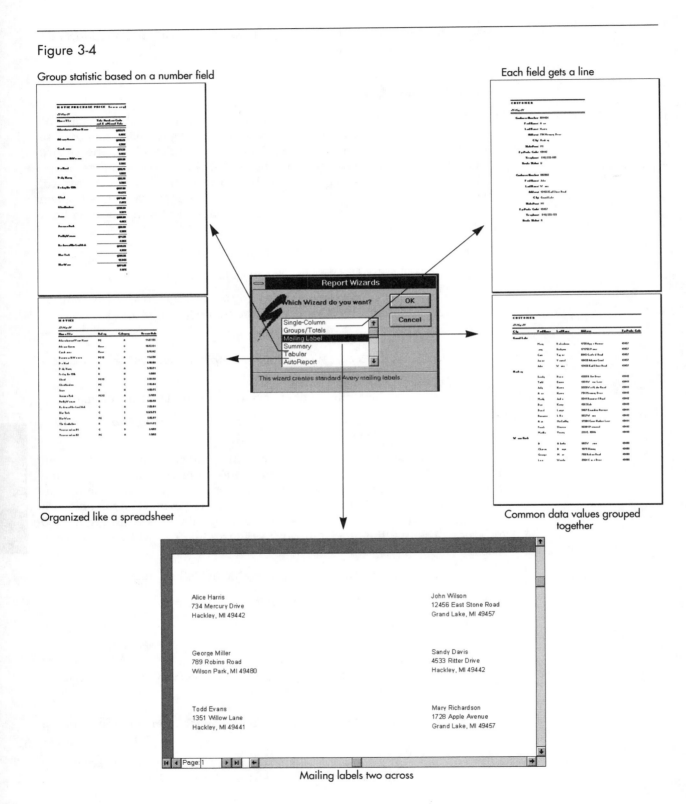

Organized like a spreadsheet

Common data values grouped together

Mailing labels two across

- Select **Last Name** in the Available fields list box.

  ▶ *The field name is highlighted.*

- Click on the single right arrow button, ⟦ › ⟧.

  ▶ *The Last Name moves to the Label appearance area.*

- Click on the New Line button.

  ▶ *The line under the First and Last Name fields is highlighted.*

P R A C T I C E   T I M E   3 - 3

Finish the mailing label design using Figure 3-5 as a guide.

1. Add the Address field to line 2.

2. Add the City, State/Prov, and Zip/Postal Code fields to the third line with a comma and space after city and at least one space between State/Prov and Zip/Postal Code.

Figure 3-5

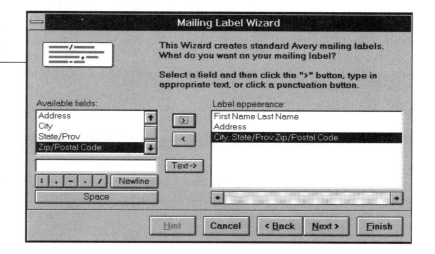

The mailing label report format is quite versatile and not limited to mailing labels. For example, given any database with people's names, this report format could be used to make name tags or labels for folders. The Text box under the Available fields list box is used to add permanent labels, like MY NAME IS, to the label. The Text button transfers the permanent label from the text box into the appearance area.

The Mailing Label wizard allows you to sort the labels and gives you the choice of several heights and widths. You also have the choice of printing one, two, or three labels across. Right now you will use the default size and spacing across the page.

- Select the Finish button.

▶   *After a pause, Access displays the report (label) design and then the print preview window with the labels, as shown at the bottom of Figure 3-4.*

NOTE: The default format might vary with 1, 2, or 3 labels displayed across the page preview.

■   Maximize the print preview window.

■   Click on the Close Window button, 🔳 .

▶   *The Report Design window is displayed.*

Saving the Report

The procedure for saving the report is the same procedure you used to save forms and queries. This time you will use the name *Customer Mailing Labels.*

■   Click on the Save button, 🔳 .

▶   *The Save As dialog box opens.*

■   Type **Customer Mailing Labels** and complete the command.

▶   *The report design window returns, as shown in Figure 3-6.*

■   Close the design window.

■   Close the window with the CUSTOMER table.

▶   *The VIDSTORE Database dialog box is displayed.*

Figure 3-6

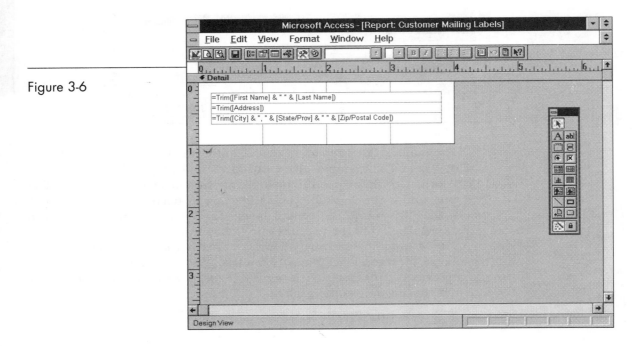

REPORT FORMATTING

Access subdivides a report into the detail section and various bands. The mailing label format you see in Figure 3-6 is the simplest type of report. It contains a **detail section** that identifies which fields from the underlying table or query are included in the report. This detail section is the mailing label design in Figure 3-6. The report design window includes both a horizontal and vertical rulers along with a tool box.

Other report types use page and report bands that contain headers and footers. Headers always precede the related footers as illustrated in Figure 3-9. In long documents, the report band would contain the title page and table of contents in the **report header** and references in the **report footer**. A page band surrounds each page. Therefore, a report will have as many page bands as pages. Column headings that match data presented in the detail section are found in **page headers.** Page numbers, dates, and customized labels can be placed in either the page header or **page footer.**

■ Select the Report tab.

▶ *The Customer Mailing Labels and other reports, if any, are listed.*

■ Choose the New button.

▶ *The New Report dialog box is displayed.*

■ Click on the Select A Table/Query down arrow.

▶ *The list of VIDSTORE tables and queries opens.*

■ Highlight **INV** (see Figure 3-7), then select the Report Wizards button.

▶ *The Report Wizards dialog box, shown earlier in Figure 3-4, opens.*

■ Select **Groups/Totals** from the list and complete the command.

▶ *The Group/Totals Report Wizard is displayed.*

Figure 3-7

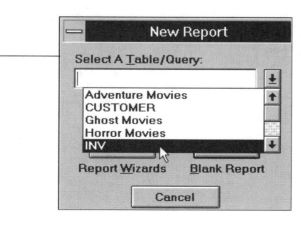

GROUP/TOTAL REPORT WIZARD

Several of the screens used by the Group/Total wizard are similar to the Mailing Label wizard you just used. You are going to use this wizard to create an Inventory Cost report that identifies how much each movie costs and how many tapes of the same movie were purchased. The records will be grouped by Movie ID and sorted by Tape Number. You will have Access compute the total purchase price for all the tapes and for each Movie ID. The final result will look like the bottom of Figure 3-9.

Figure 3-8

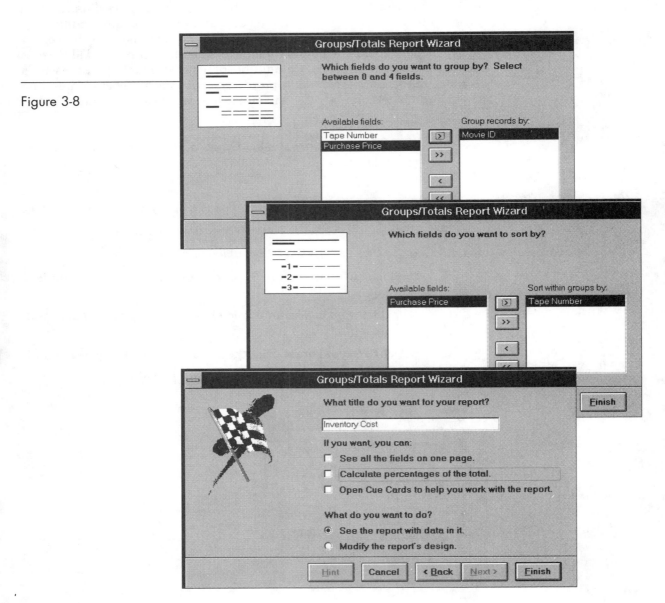

- Use the single arrow key (▶) to move the **Tape Number**, **Movie ID**, and **Purchase Price** to the Field order on the report list box.

- Select the <u>N</u>ext button.

  ▶   *The wizard displays a dialog box that asks you to group data.*

- Move **Movie ID** to the Group records list box (see Figure 3-8) and select <u>N</u>ext.

  ▶   *The wizard asks how you want to group data.*

- With Normal in the Group text box, select <u>N</u>ext.

  ▶   *The wizard wants to know which field to sort by in the Movie ID group.*

- Move **Tape Number** to the Sort within groups by list box (see Figure 3-8) and select <u>N</u>ext.

  ▶   *The wizard displays different formatting options.*

Page Orientation

The Group/Total wizard lets you choose from three different preset report formats: Executive, Presentation, and Ledger. You will use the default and make sure that a portrait orientation is used. A ***portrait*** orientation means that Access uses an 8.5" by 11" page layout that is taller than it is wide. The other orientation, ***landscape***, uses an 11" by 8.5" page layout that is wider than it is tall.

- Choose the **Portrait** button and select <u>N</u>ext.

  ▶   *The last wizard window where you can change the report title is displayed.*

- Delete INV in the report title area and type **Inventory Costs**.

- Click on X in front of Calculate percentages of total.

  ▶   *The check box is cleared, as shown at the bottom of Figure 3-8.*

- Select the <u>F</u>inish button.

  ▶   *After a long pause, Access displays the report design and then a print preview, as shown in part at the bottom of Figure 3-9.*

- Maximize the print preview design window.

The report is several pages long, with a grand total appearing on the last page.

Figure 3-9

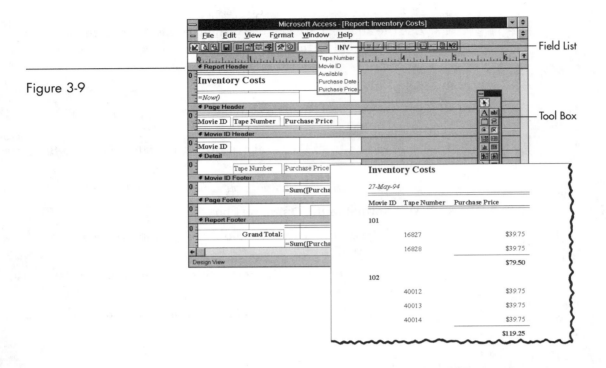

Field List

Tool Box

PRACTICE TIME 3-4

1. Return the display to the report design window by closing the print preview window.

2. Save the report using the name **Inventory Costs**. Your screen should look like the top of Figure 3-9 except for the appearance of the field list and toolbox.

3. If necessary, use the Field List button (▦) to close the INV field list.

4. If necessary, use the Toolbox button (▨) to close the toolbox.

MODIFYING THE REPORT DESIGN

The report wizard has accomplished a considerable amount of work while you waited. Take another look at the report design in Figure 3-9. In the report header under the title Inventory Costs is the =Now() *function* that returns the current date. This is one of several built-in functions that perform tasks and place the results in an Access object where the function name is located. A few examples from over 150 different Access functions are listed in Table 1. The =Sum function in the report footer displays the results of adding the purchase price from each record together. These results are labeled Grand Total.

TABLE 1   Commonly Used Access Functions

Function	Description
Avg	Calculates the arithmetic mean of a set of values contained in a specified field on a query, table, or form.
Count	Calculates the number of selected records in a query, table, or form.
CurrentUser	Returns the name of the current Access user.
Date	Returns the current date.
Log	Returns the natural logarithm of a number.
Now	Returns the current date and time.
Page	Calculates a report page number.
Pmt	Returns the payment on an annuity based on periodic, constant payments and a constant interest rate.
Rate	Returns the interest rate per period for an annuity.
Rnd	Returns a random number.
Sgn	Returns a value indicating the sign (+, -, 0) of a number.
Sin	Returns the sine of an angle.
Sqr	Returns the square root of a number.
StDev	Returns an estimate of the standard deviation of a population or population sample represented as a set of values contained in a specified field on a query, table, or form.
Sum	Returns the sum of a set of values contained in a specified field on a query, table, or form.
Tan	Returns the tangent of an angle.
Time$	Returns the current time in a 24-hour format.
Timer	Returns the number of seconds that have elapsed since 12:00 A.M. (midnight).
Var	Returns estimates of the variance of a population or population sample represented as a set of values contained in a specified field on a query, table, or form.

Each page starts with a page header that contains column labels for the Movie ID, Tape Number, and Purchase Price. The related page footer uses the =Page function to display the current page number.

Changing Field Properties

One correction that needs to be made to this design involves the Purchase Price label in the page header. Since the purchase price is a right-aligned number field, the related column label should also be right-aligned. Before realigning the column label, let's check the ***property sheet*** box to see the default setting.

■   Click on Purchase Price in the Page Header.

▶ *A border with eight boxes, called sizing handles, surrounds the label.*

■ From the View menu, select Properties.

Alternative: Use the Properties button, 🖼 .

▶ *The property sheet that displays the highlighted label's attributes opens.*

NOTE: A property sheet is also activated by clicking once using the right mouse button to open the control menu and then selecting the Properties option.

■ Click on the property sheet's title bar and drag the box to the right, as shown in Figure 9-10.

▶ *The property sheet's location onscreen changes.*

■ Scroll the list box down until you see the Text Align property.

▶ *The default test alignment is General.*

■ Click on the word General.

▶ *The down arrow is displayed at the right side of the list box.*

■ Open the list box by selecting the down arrow.

▶ *The text alignment options are listed, as shown in Figure 3-10.*

■ Select Right.

▶ *The Text Align changes to Right, and the related list box closes.*

Figure 3-10

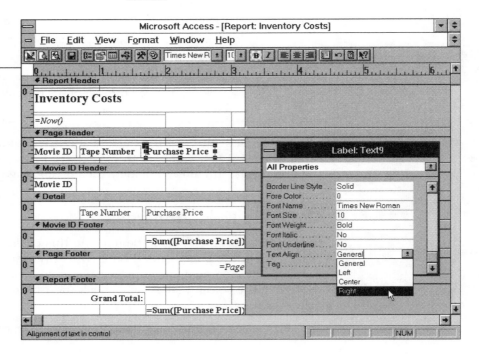

Adjusting Display Formats

The ***label box*** assigned to the words Purchase Price needs to be wider so it is even with the purchase price data displayed in the Detail section. It is called a label box because it holds a description, like the report title, that does not change when the report is updated. ***Text boxes*** are areas of the report which contain data from a table or query. Data in these boxes could change every time the report design is opened. Movie ID in the Page Header is in a text box.

You move or adjust the size of either box type by using the ***sizing handles*** that surround an active box. In Figure 3-10 the Purchase Price label box is active. Pressing the Delete key at this time removes the field from the report. When the pointer is inside the active box, it is an insertion pointer. Clicking the mouse here allows you to add or delete text or field names.

As you move the pointer over the lines connecting the sizing handles it changes to a hand pointer, 🖐. Moving the pointer over the ***move handle***, which is in the top left corner of the active box, turns the pointer into a pointing hand, 👆 . When either the hand or pointing hand pointer is active, you can move the field to a new location in the report. For example, you could move the page number from the page footer to the page header. Traditional cut and paste procedures also accomplish the same thing.

To widen the Purchase Price label, you will use the sizing pointer (↔) to drag the right side of the box to a new location. When placement precision is called for, the ruler line can be consulted when repositioning an object. You will move the right side of the box until it is on the 3-inch mark of the horizontal ruler.

■ Move the pointer over the middle sizing handle to the right of Purchase Price.

▶ *The pointer changes into a horizontal sizing pointer,* ↔ .

■ Click and drag the sizing handle to the right until it is over the light gray layout line.

▶ *Access highlights the horizontal ruler to the 3-inch mark.*

■ Release the mouse.

▶ *The Purchase Price label is right-aligned 3 inches from the left margin.*

PRACTICE TIME 3-5

1. Adjust the right side of the Purchase Price text box in the Detail section to align with the 3-inch mark on the horizontal ruler.

2. Print the preview report. If necessary, return to the design window to make further adjustments until the Purchase Price and the related column label line up.

3. Close the print preview.

DATABASE

Group Headers and Footers

In addition to page and report bands, the Group/Total wizard adds group bands to the report design. Group bands are divided into headers and footers like the other bands. When displayed, a group band subdivides the detail section into related categories based on values within a designated field. The Inventory Costs report uses a group band based on the Movie ID field. As a result, records with a common Movie ID are grouped together. The =Sum function in the Movie ID Footer adds together all the purchase prices for video tapes of the same movie.

Even the width of a header and footer can be modified. You just drag it up to shorten the width and drag it down to widen it.

P R A C T I C E   T I M E   3 - 6

1. Adjust the right side of the =Sum text box in the Movie ID Footer to align with the 3-inch mark on the horizontal ruler.

2. Print the preview report. If necessary, return to the design window to make further adjustments until the =Sum and Purchase Price text boxes line up.

3. Close the print preview.

4. Close the report design window and save any changes.

TWO-TABLE QUERY

It is easy creating reports using Access wizards. The hard part is making sure the report design is easy to use. The Inventory Costs report is an example of a report that provides the information you need but is difficult to use. The main reason for this is the use of Movie ID as a group identifier. While it is good database design to have a unique identifier for each movie, people using the report would be more comfortable using the movie title. The two report formats are compared in Figure 3-11.

Movie titles were not used because the related field is in the MOVIES table, not in the INV table used for the Inventory Costs report. However, combining data from two tables is not a problem for a relational database as long as both tables have at least one field in common. In this case the Movie ID field occurs in both the MOVIES and the INV tables. Therefore, the Movie ID field would be the *join field* (common field) between both tables.

To make the Inventory Costs report easier to read, you will create a query that includes the Movie ID, Tape Number, and Purchase Price from the INV table and the Movie Title from the MOVIES table. You can then use this two-table query instead of the INV table as the underlying source of data for the report.

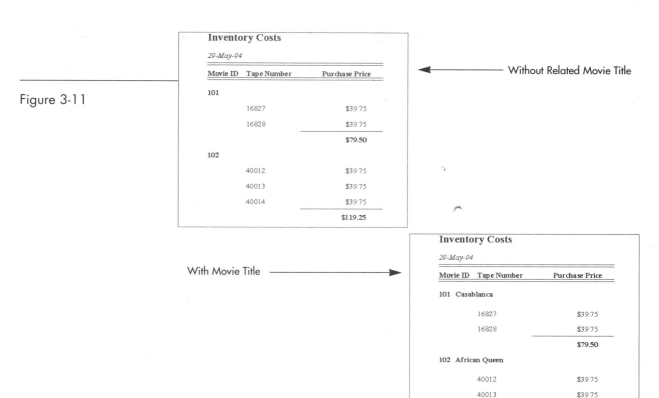

Figure 3-11

Without Related Movie Title

With Movie Title

■ From the VIDSTORE Database dialog box, select the Query tab.

▶ *Adventure Movies and other queries are displayed.*

■ Choose the New button.

▶ *The New Query dialog box is displayed.*

■ Select the New Query button.

▶ *The query design window and the Add Table dialog box open.*

■ Highlight **INV** and choose the Add button.

▶ *The INV field list is added to the query design.*

■ Highlight **MOVIES** and select the Add button.

▶ *The MOVIES field list is added to the query design.*

■ Close the Add Table dialog box.

When possible, Access identifies a join field in common to both tables that can serve as a link between the two. As discussed earlier, the Movie ID field is the join field in this case. Access draws a line between the field names when identifying the join field. This link can be seen between the Movie ID fields of the INV and MOVIES table in the field list area of Figure 3-12.

DATABASE

Figure 3-12

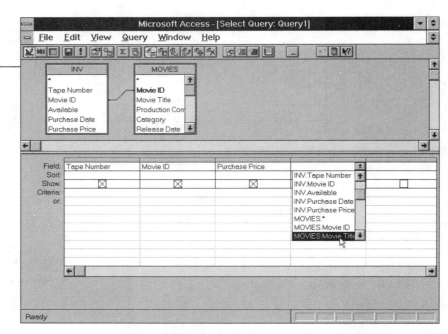

When two or more tables are used, Access precedes the field name with the table name. Therefore, the Tape Number field in the INV table is referenced as INV.Tape Number. In Figure 3-12, the Movie Title field name appears in the list box as MOVIES.Movie title.

P R A C T I C E   T I M E   3 - 7

Use Figure 3-12 as a guide.

1. Add INV.Tape Number to the first Field area in the QBE grid.

2. Add INV.Movie ID to the second Field area.

3. Add INV.Purchase Price to the third field area.

4. Add MOVIES.Movie title to the fourth field area.

5. Save the query using the query name **Inventory Costs**.

6. Close the query design window.

LINKING A REPORT TO A DIFFERENT SOURCE

Report data can be drawn from either a table or query. You can easily reassign a report to a different source using the design window's property sheet. Since the Inventory Costs query contains the Movie Title along with the other data used by the report, it should be used as a data source instead of the INV table.

■ From the VIDSTORE Database dialog box, select the Report tab.

▶ *Inventory Costs and other reports are displayed.*

■ Highlight Inventory Costs and select the <u>D</u>esign button.

▶ *The Inventory Costs design window opens.*

■ Display the active field list by clicking on the Field List button, 🔲 .

▶ *The field names from the INV table are listed.*

■ If necessary, display the property sheet using the Properties button, 🖳 .

▶ *The property sheet's title bar displays Report.*

NOTE: If the property sheet's title bar references some other label or text box, click on an unused report area to have the property sheet display general report attributes.

■ Click to the right of INV in the Record Source area of the property sheet.

▶ *An insertion point and a down arrow appear.*

■ Select the down arrow and highlight Inventory Costs, as shown in Figure 3-13.

▶ *The Inventory Costs query is reassigned as the Record Source, and the Inventory Costs field list is displayed.*

Figure 3-13

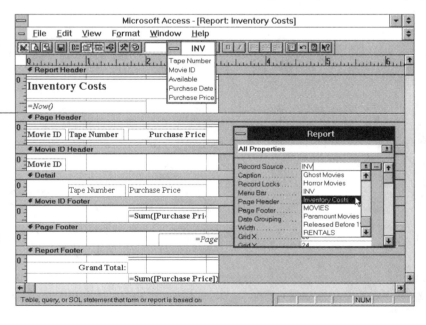

Adding a Field to the Report Design

All you need to do to finish the report modification is to drag the Movie Title field name from the field list box into the Movie ID header. You will also fine tune the design by shortening the width of the Movie ID text box. The Movie Title text box will also need to be widened in order to fit the longest movie name.

P R A C T I C E   T I M E   3 - 8

Adjust the right side of the Movie ID text box in the Movie ID Header to align with the 1/4 inch mark on the horizontal ruler. *Hint:* As shown in Figure 3-14, only *Mo* of Movie ID can be seen in the text box when the size is adjusted properly.

■ Drag the Movie Title from the field list into the Movie ID Header to the immediate right of the Movie ID text box.

▶ *The placement of the Movie Title should be similar to Figure 3-14.*

■ Drag the middle sizing handle to the right until it is over the light gray layout line, as shown in Figure 3-14.

▶ *Access highlights the horizontal ruler to 2-inch mark.*

■ Save the report.

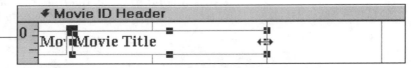

Figure 3-14

Printing a Report

All that is left to do is to print the report. Since it is several pages long, your instructor might want you to print only a few pages. If this is the case, use the pages option in the Print dialog box.

■ Make sure the printer is on and ready to print.

■ Click on the Print Preview button.

▶ *A preview of the report is displayed, as shown at the bottom of Figure 9-11.*

■ Print the report by clicking on the Print button, 🖨.

▶ *The Print dialog box opens.*

You printed the full report earlier by simply completing the command—either clicking on OK or pressing Enter. To try something different,

Figure 3-15

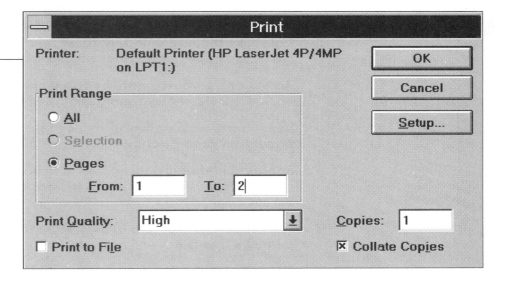

let's print pages 1 and 2 only, as shown in Figure 3-15.

■ Select the Pages button in the Print Range area.

▶ *An insertion point appears in the From text box.*

■ Type **1** and press TAB.

▶ *The insertion point jumps to the To text box.*

■ Type **2**.

▶ *The Print dialog box looks like Figure 3-15.*

■ Complete the command.

▶ *Access prints the first two pages of the report.*

ENDING LESSON 3

There are many more features of an Access report such as adding presentation graphics, internal computations, and an assortment of document design features. These should be explored on your own. Just remember that the only way to learn to use a database management system is by trying it.

This is the end of Lesson 3. Close all open windows and exit Access. If you are done with the computer, follow the recommended procedures for shutting down the computer system.

■ Close all open Access windows.

■ Exit Access.

SUMMARY

❏ **Database tables created by other relational database systems can be imported or attached to an Access database.**

❏ **Access users create printed documents using different report wizards. Data comes from designated tables or queries.**

❏ **Reports are automatically divided into a detail section, page band, and report band.**

❏ **Special built-in functions perform tasks that insert the current date, averages, sums, or record counts into an Access object.**

❏ **The property sheet box allows users to see and change default settings.**

❏ **The sizing and move handles associated with the active field of a report can be used to fine tune the physical size and placement of the field.**

❏ **A group band organizes records into subgroups based on specific field values. These bands are added or deleted at any time.**

❏ **Queries can use data from several fields and join multiple tables.**

KEY TERMS

attaching	landscape	report footer
detail section	move handle	report header
function	page footer	sizing handles
import	page header	text box
join field	portrait	
label box	property sheet	

COMMAND SUMMARY

REVIEW QUESTIONS

1. What is the difference between importing and attaching a table to an Access database?

2. In what ways are reports designed to be different from queries?

3. What does the New Report Wizard do?

4. Identify three applications for the mailing label report format.

5. What report formatting features are supported by the detail section, page bands, and report band?

6. What Access functions insert the current date and page number into a report and compute a group total?

7. How are report properties changed?

8. How do you adjust the display size or location of a field in a report?

9. What type of information would be found in a group band?

10. What is needed to link data from two tables into a single query dynaset?

11. How do you reassign a report to a different table or query?

12. How are new fields added to a report?

EXERCISES

1. Use your FRIENDS table in the PERSONAL database to create mailing labels and track birthdays.

   a. Create and print mailing labels for friends and family.

   b. Develop a query called **September Birthdays** that identifies all September birthdays. Include in the dynaset data the Name, Telephone, and Birthday fields. Sort dynaset in ascending order by birthday. Print the dynaset.

   c. Prepare and print a report called **Birthdays**. The report should be based on the September Birthdays query. The report should include the following headings:

   SEPTEMBER BIRTHDAYS   **Today's Date**

   The report itself must use the following data fields in the detail section in this order: Name, Telephone, Birthday (99/99/99 format).

2. Track your earnings and organize your files using your STOCKS table in the BUSINESS database.

   a. Prepare and print a report called HOLDINGS detailing your stock portfolio (STOCKS). The report should have the following data in the detail section: Stock Name, Number of Shares, and Current Share Price.

   b. Create and print mailing labels for all your stock holdings. These labels will be used as folder tags for annual reports and other paper correspondences. Use the mailing label format shown below.

Stock Name - Transaction Number

Date Purchased

c. Develop and print a report called **Holdings** that lists your current stock holdings. The report contains a grand total of the number of shares purchased. The report heading should include your name and today's date in the following format:

***Your Name's* CURRENT STOCK HOLDINGS   Today's Date**

The following data should be included in the detail section in this order: Stock Name, Number of Shares, Purchase Price, Current Price.

3. Use your SUPPLIERS table in the VIDSTORE database to create a report and mailing labels.

a. Prepare and print a report called **Supplier Balances** that shows all the supplier names and balances.

b. Develop a two-table query called **Inventory List** using the MOVIES and INV tables. The Movie ID field is the link between the two tables. The dynaset includes the following fields: Movie Title, Category, Rating, and Tape Number. Sort dynaset by Movie Title and Tape Number.

c. Develop and print a report called **Inventory List** based on the Inventory List query that uses the following fields in the detail section: Movie Title, Tape Number, Category, Rating.

d. Use Mailing Label wizard to prepare and print mailing labels of all suppliers. Mailing labels should be printed two across.

e. Save the mailing labels report as **Supplier Labels**.

4 Enhancing Database Applications

OBJECTIVES

Upon completing the material presented in this lesson, you should understand the following aspects of Access:

❑ **Sorting data in a table**

❑ **Filtering data**

❑ **Adding an index**

❑ **Creating Reports with the AutoReport Wizard**

❑ **Developing and Running Macros**

❑ **Using Parameter Queries**

STARTING OFF

Turn on your computer, start Windows, and then launch the Access 2.0 for Windows program as you did in previous lessons. Insert your data disk and set the working directory if necessary. Maximize the Access application window.

- Insert your data disk into the disk drive.
- Launch Access.

  ▶   *The Access application window is displayed.*

- Open the VIDSTORE database.
- If necessary, maximize the application window.

SORTING AND FILTERING TABLE RECORDS

You will find that tables are the foundation from which database applications grow. Queries then draw from one or more tables to organize data into usable information. Many of the ways you manipulate data in a query through sorting and selection criteria can be applied directly to data in a table. As a result, a question often arises as to when it is appropriate to create and save a new query dynaset rather than directly manipulating the data in the table.

When to Use a Table

Sorting records into ascending order by movie title or just displaying adventure movies does not require a query. It makes the most sense to manipulate the database table as a datasheet when two situations occur:

1. All the data you need is confined to a single table.

2. The need for data in this arrangement is not likely to occur again.

When to Use a Query

New queries are developed when they help to answer often-asked questions. In these situations, the query can be saved and opened again whenever it is needed. Having the query saved on disk is better than saving a printed copy of the results because the most up-to-date data is used every time the query is opened and run. Printed data can easily become obsolete when the database is constantly being updated. Relying on the disk-based query also provides an additional benefit of reducing the paper clutter that surrounds most desks. Many times a new dynaset may only need to be displayed, not printed.

Queries also work best when the data you need is found in different tables. Queries using data from two or more tables are examined later in the lesson.

Quick Sort

Records are maintained in a table in either key field order or, if a primary key is missing, in the order they were entered. Using the Quick Sort feature to sort records into another order is only maintained until the table is closed or until the records are sorted again. Therefore, any change you make to the order in which records are displayed in a table is temporary. Quick Sort reorganizes the datasheet based on data values in the currently active field. The active field is the one with the flashing insertion point or highlighted field data.

- Open the MOVIES table.

- Click on the first movie title.

    ▶ *An insertion point appears in Casablanca, or the movie title is highlighted.*

- From the Records menu, select Quick Sort.

    Alternative: Use the Sort Ascending button (🔼) or Sort Descending button (🔽).

    ▶ *A secondary menu opens with Ascending and Descending options (see top of Figure 4-1).*

- Choose Ascending.

    ▶ *The MOVIES datasheet sorts by movie title, as shown in the bottom of Figure 4-1.*

Figure 4-1

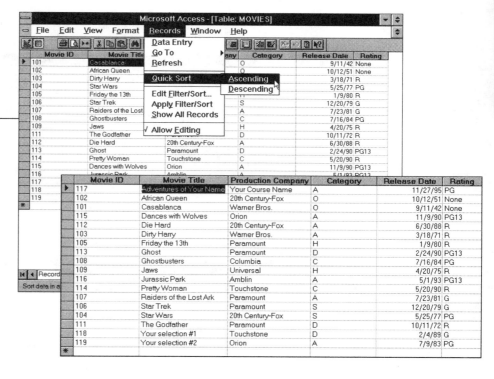

Data Filters

Many of the selection features of a query's QBE grid can be applied to a table's datasheet display as a *filter*. As the name implies, filters are used to selectively display data. To do so requires a selection criterion that works the same as the criterion used in a query. Therefore, it should be of no surprise that the Filter window in Figure 4-2 looks just like a Select Query window.

■   From the <u>R</u>ecords menu, choose Edit <u>F</u>ilter/Sort.

Alternative: Use the Edit Filter/Sort button, 🔳 .

▶   *The Filter window opens.*

Notice the grid already contains the Movie Title field name and Ascending in the Sort area. These options were added to the grid when you used the Quick Sort feature. To limit the datasheet display to adventure movies, you will add the Category field name to the grid and the expression "A" to the Criteria area.

■   Add the Category field name to the Field area to the right of Movie Title.

■   Type **"A"** in the Criteria area below Category.

▶   *The Filter window should look like the top of Figure 4-2.*

■   From the <u>R</u>ecords menu, choose Appl<u>y</u> Filter/Sort.

Alternative: Use the Apply Filter/Sort button, 🔳 .

▶   *The datasheet displays only adventure movies, as shown in the bottom of Figure 4-2.*

Figure 4-2

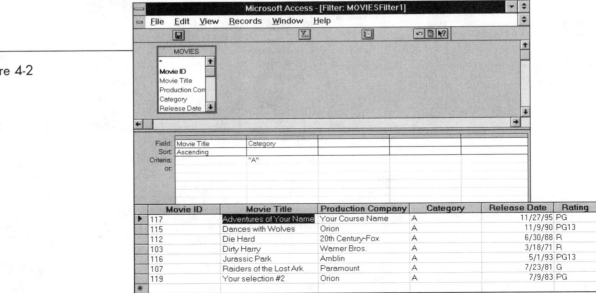

To turn off all filters and sort options, you select <u>S</u>how All Records from the <u>R</u>ecords menu. This menu option returns the datasheet back to the original settings.

■   From the <u>R</u>ecords menu, select <u>S</u>how All Records.

   Alternative: Use Show All Records button, 🖼 .

   ▶   *The datasheet displays all the records in Movie ID order.*

P R A C T I C E   T I M E   4 - 1

1. Sort the MOVIES datasheet into ascending order by release date.

2. Display only PG or PG13 rated movies.

3. Print the sorted datasheet with currently active filters.

4. Show all records.

INDEXING A TABLE

As the number of records in a table increases, it takes more time to complete a Quick Sort. To speed up sorting and searching of commonly used fields, you can create an ***index*** for the field in question using the table design window. In the MOVIES table, the Movie Title field would be an ideal index because it is often the basis for a query and the logical order for reports based on the MOVIES table. The Last Name field in the CUSTOMER table would be another good field to index. To start, you will create an index for the Release Date field.

■   Click on the Design button, 🖼 .

   ▶   *The report design window opens.*

■   Activate the row selector to the left of Release Date

   ▶   *The Release Date field name, type, and description are highlighted, as shown in Figure 4-3.*

Since it is possible for two movies to have the same release date, duplicate values of this index field are acceptable. If the no duplicates option is selected, Access will not allow the same release date to be entered for different movies.

■   At the bottom of the screen in Field Properties pane, click in the text box to the right of Indexed.

   ▶   *An insertion point and a down arrow appear.*

Figure 4-3

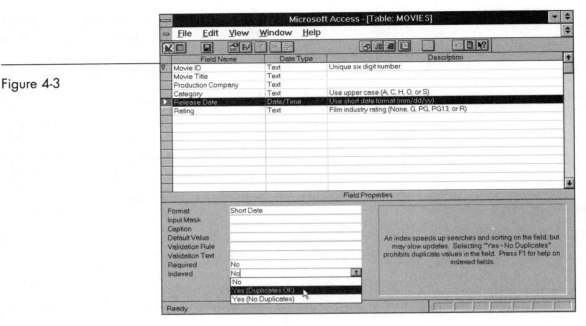

■   Click on the down arrow.

▶   *A list of index options opens, as shown in Figure 4-3.*

■   Select **Yes (Duplicates OK)**.

▶   *The index qualifications are added to the table design.*

Create an index only when searching and sorting speeds need to be improved. Establishing new indexes creates new files that must be updated every time a record is added or deleted from a table. As a result, data entry is often slowed down when a table contains several indexes. Therefore, when adding a new index, the loss of speed during data entry must be weighed against speed gains in sorting and searching.

Removing an Index

When adding an index does not produce expected performance gains or when new indexes bog down data entry, consider removing the index. This is easily accomplished using the Indexes window and Delete key.

■   From the table design window, open the <u>V</u>iew menu, and select Indexes.

▶   *Access opens the Indexes:MOVIES window.*

This window lists all the active indexes for a table and allows users to change the index's sort order.

■   Activate the row selector for Release Date.

▶   *The Release Date index is highlighted, as shown in Figure 4-4.*

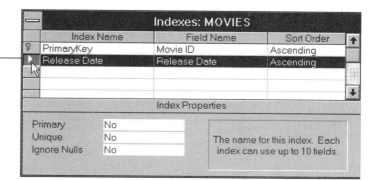

Figure 4-4

- Press Delete.

  Alternative: Use the right mouse button to open the shortcut menu and select Delete Row.

  ▶   *The Release Date index is removed from the table.*

- Close the MOVIES indexes window.

  ▶   *The display returns to the report design window.*

PRACTICE TIME 4-2

Using the MOVIES table, establish Movie Titles as an index field where duplicate titles are acceptable.

QUERY JOINING FOUR TABLES

A two-day limit on video rentals is the current store policy. Boomtown's management periodically needs to identify tape rentals that have been out over two days. You will use Access to create a Late Tape Call List. It will identify the customer's name, telephone number, the movie's title, and the tape's replacement cost. The data necessary for this query must be drawn from all four tables (MOVIES, CUSTOMER, INV, and RENTALS). The resulting dynaset is shown later in this lesson as a part of Figure 4-9. It is based on a query that identifies the following data and links between tables:

- Customer name and telephone number comes from the CUSTOMER table.

- Customer number links the CUSTOMER and RENTALS tables.

- The RENTALS table provides the date the tape was rented—Date Out. An empty Date In field identifies unreturned rentals.

- The tape number from the RENTALS table serves as a link to the INV tables.
- The tape's original purchase price is found in the INV table.
- The Movie ID number is the link between the INV and MOVIES tables.
- The movie title is obtained from the MOVIES table.

Joining Tables

If the database tables have been designed to integrate together, like VID-STORE, creating a query based on data from four tables is straightforward.

■ Close all open windows except for the VIDSTORE database window. This window should be maximized.

■ Select the Query button.

▶ *The Query list with Adventure Movies and other queries you created earlier is displayed.*

■ Choose the New button.

▶ *The New Query dialog box is displayed.*

■ Select the New Query button.

▶ *The Add Table dialog box opens with the select query design window in the background.*

■ Choose CUSTOMER, then select the Add button.

▶ *The CUSTOMER field list is inserted above the QBE grid.*

As you add the other tables to the query Access will attempt to establish join lines between each table. As shown in Figure 4-5, a ***join line*** is automatically drawn between the two tables when a link is found. The line connects the field names of the fields common to both tables. Bold field names identify the table's primary key. You can manually create join lines between tables by dragging the pointer from the field name in one list to a compatible field name in another list.

P R A C T I C E   T I M E   4 - 3

Add the following tables to the query in this order: RENTALS, INV, and MOVIES. Use the scroll bar to bring all the joined tables into view. When you are done, the screen should look like Figure 4-5.

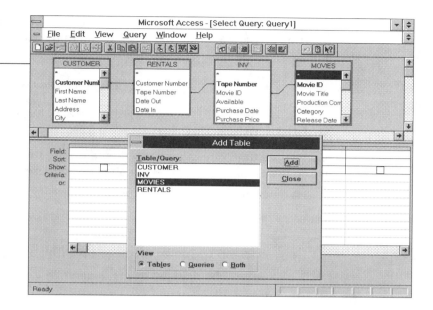

Figure 4-5

Referential Integrity

It is no coincidence that the primary key in each of the tables is used to join records in one table to records in other tables. Good relational database design depends on key fields that uniquely define a record. For example, the Movie ID field is the MOVIES Table's primary key. Movie ID 101 uniquely identifies Casablanca, its release date, rating, and so on. The Movie ID also joins the MOVIES table to the INV table which allows you to match these data with the purchase price and other data about a specific tape.

However, this link between the two tables can be easily corrupted if *referential integrity* is lost. This would be the case if you deleted the Casablanca record from the MOVIES table. Then, the INV table would have tape records that refer to Movie ID 101 when there would no longer be any record in the MOVIES table with a matching Movie ID. Referential integrity would be lost. Therefore, to maintain referential integrity, fields that join tables in a relational database should not be deleted as long as links to other tables still exist.

Two basic rules should be followed for a database to maintain referential integrity:

1. You cannot add a record in a joined table until a record with an acceptable primary key field value is present. In other words, you could not enter a new INV record until an acceptable Movie ID existed in the MOVIES table.

2. You cannot delete a record with a primary key from a table when matching records still exist in other tables. This means you must delete all the Casablanca tapes from the INV table before the Movie ID 101 record can be deleted from the MOVIES table.

DATABASE

Access maintains referential integrity when asked to enforce it. In this case, an error message is displayed when either of the two conditions above exist.

■   Close the Add Table dialog box.

▶   *The select query design window is displayed.*

Multiple Table Query

When more than one table is used by a query, the field list identifies fields by the table name.field name, as shown in Figure 4-6.

■   Click in the first Field area.

▶   *An insertion point and a down arrow appear in the Field area.*

■   Click on the down arrow to open the field list.

▶   *The field list opens, as shown in Figure 4-6.*

■   Select CUSTOMER.First Name.

▶   *First Name is added to the QBE grid.*

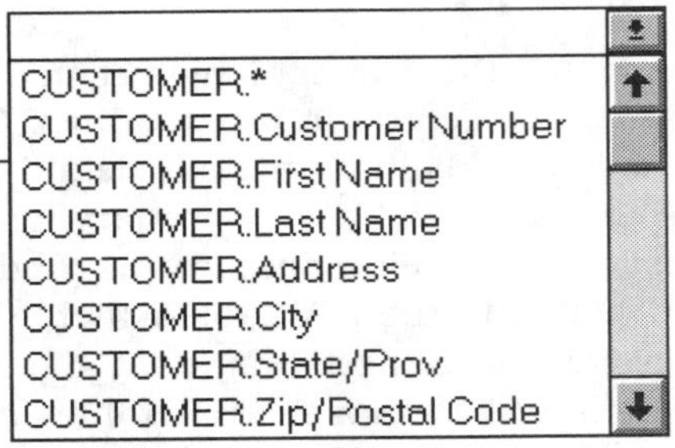

Figure 4-6

```
CUSTOMER.*
CUSTOMER.Customer Number
CUSTOMER.First Name
CUSTOMER.Last Name
CUSTOMER.Address
CUSTOMER.City
CUSTOMER.State/Prov
CUSTOMER.Zip/Postal Code
```

Fields are also added to the query dynaset by dragging the field name from a field list down into a QBE grid Field area.

PRACTICE TIME 4-4

1. Add the following fields to the QBE grid in this order: Last Name, Telephone, Date Out, Date In, Movie Title, and Purchase Price. Use the scroll box to display empty field areas that are currently offscreen.

2. Turn off the Show option for the Date Out and Date In fields.

3. Sort the dynaset in ascending order by Last Name.

4. Save the query using **Late Tape Call List** as the query name.

When you are done, the QBE grid should look like Figure 4-7. Please note that the Field area columns have been adjusted in this Figure to show all fields. Some fields may be scrolled off your screen display.

Field:	First Name	Last Name	Telephone	Date Out	Date In	Movie Title	Purchase Price
Sort:		Ascending					
Show:	☒	☒	☒	☐	☐	☒	☒
Criteria:							
or:							

Figure 4-7

Null Fields

Two conditions must exist before we add someone to the late tape dynaset. First, the Date In field must be empty. Access uses a special criteria, **null**, to identify empty fields. In this situation you will add *Is Null* to the Date In Criteria.

■ Type **is null** to the Date In Criteria area.

▶ *Adds search criteria to QBE grid as shown in Figure 4-9.*

Using Dates In Computations

The second condition that must exist is that the Date Out must be over two days—the store's definition of a late tape. Since Access treats dates as sequential numbers, it is possible to subtract 2 from the current date. Any Date Out smaller than today's date minus 2 identifies a tape that was rented over two days ago. The Now() function identifies the current date. Left and right parentheses without any spaces in between are part of the Now() function. Therefore, the search criteria *<Now()-2* will identify late tapes if the Date In is null.

■ Type **<Now()-2** in the Date Out Criteria area.

▶ *Search criteria are added to the QBE grid, as shown in Figure 4-9.*

The Expression Builder

The last field in the query is purchase price. This is the price Boomtown originally paid for the tape. If the tape needs to be replaced, the customer will actually be charged an additional 10% to compensate the store for time and effort. Access's Expression Builder, see Figure 4-8, is used to place a formula within an object. A new field name, Replacement Cost, is created by multiplying Purchase Price by 1.1. This formula increases the Purchase Price by 10 percent.

■ Click on the Purchase Price field name using the right mouse button.

Alternative: With an insertion point in the desired field, select the Builder button, [···].

DATABASE

▶   *The Shortcut menu opens.*

■   Select the Build option.

▶   *The Expression Builder dialog box opens with the Purchase Price in the expression area.*

■   Click in the expression area and move the insertion point to the left of Purchase Price.

■   Type **Replacement Cost:[** (no space after left bracket).

NOTE: Do not confuse the left and right brackets [] with left and right parentheses.

■   Move the insertion point to the right of Purchase Price and type **]*1.1** (no space at end).

▶   *The formula in the expression area should look like Figure 4-8.*

Expression area

Figure 4-8

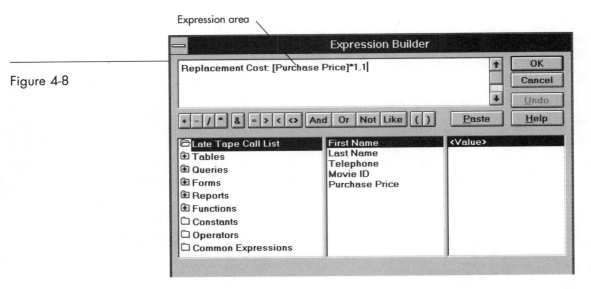

■   Complete the command.

▶   *The display returns to the select query design window, as shown at the top of Figure 4-9.*

■   Run the query.

▶   *The dynaset looks like the bottom of Figure 4-9.*

Figure 4-9

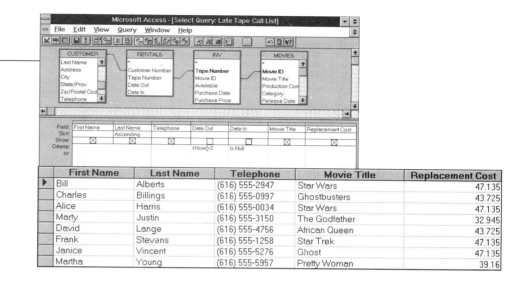

P R A C T I C E   T I M E   4 - 5

1. Save the current version of Late Tape Call List query.

2. Close the select query design window.

AUTOREPORT WIZARD

The Late Tape Call List will be a single column report you will create using the Auto Report Wizard. If the Late Tape Call List query is highlighted in the database dialog box, the wizard automatically creates the report using field names from the designated object.

■   Make sure the Late Tape Call List is highlighted in the Query list of the VIDSTORE database dialog box.

■   Click on the Auto Report tool button, ▨ .

▶   *After a long pause while Access creates the new report, it then displays the report in the print preview window.*

■   Maximize the window.

Notice that the Replacement Cost field should be left aligned and in a currency format. These changes to the way Replacement Cost is displayed can be made by using the report design window, as shown in Figure 4-10.

■   Close the print preview window.

▶   *The report design window is displayed.*

Figure 4-10

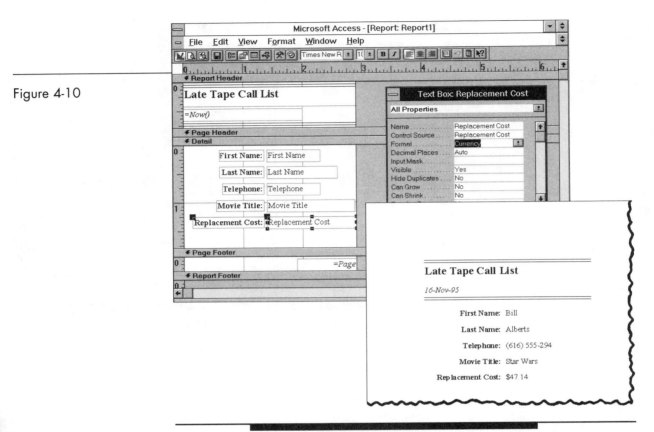

PRACTICE TIME 4-6

1. Use the Replacement Cost properties window to change Format to **Currency** (see Figure 4-10) and Text align to **Left**.

2. Save the report as Late Tape Call List.

3. Close the report design window.

MACROS

The VIDSTORE database is made up of several Access *objects*. Tables, queries, forms, reports, macros, and modules represent different object types. Yet to be discussed are macros and modules. **Macros** are a set of commands users enter to automate routine or repetitive tasks, like the steps to print a report. **Modules** are complete computer programs written in Access's native command language. You would recognize some of these commands, like Open, because they are also menu options. Writing programs using Access commands is beyond the scope of this book.

On the other hand, macros are quick and easy to create. To help streamline procedures for printing the Late Tape Calling List, you will create a macro that automatically opens the report, prints it, and then closes the report.

■ From the VIDSTORE database window, select the Macro tab.

▶ *An empty Macros list opens.*

■ Select the <u>N</u>ew button.

▶ *Access displays the macro window.*

Creating a Macro

You will add action commands to the macro as shown in Figure 4-13. These commands are selected from a list box. Associated comments can be added to the Comment line to the right of the command. While these comments are ignored by Access, they make it easier for users to understand each macro step.

■ Click in the first row of the Action column.

▶ *An insertion point and a down arrow appear in the first action area.*

■ Select the down arrow.

▶ *The list of macro commands opens.*

■ Scroll down the list until OpenReport is found (see Figure 4-11).

■ Select **OpenReport**.

▶ *The OpenReport command is added to the first action area.*

Figure 4-11

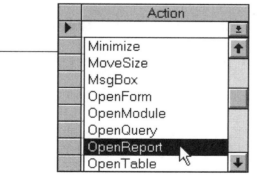

Once an action has been identified, Access prompts the selection of Action Arguments in the lower portion of the screen. These arguments identify specific objects, views, filters, and selection criteria that clarify the command. You will identify two arguments: Report Name and View. The Late Tape Call List is the report. Print preview will be the view.

DATABASE

■   Click in the open area to the right of Report Name.

▶   *An insertion point and a down arrow appear in argument area.*

■   Click on the down area and select **Late Tape Call List**.

▶   *The report name is added to the argument area, as shown in Figure 4-12.*

■   If necessary, click in the View argument area, choose the down arrow, and select **Print Preview**.

▶   *The Print Preview is added to the argument area.*

Argument area

Figure 4-12

Report Name	Late Tape Call List
View	Print Preview
Filter Name	
Where Condition	

PRACTICE TIME 4-7

1. Insert the **Print** command in the second action row.

2. Insert the **Close** command in the third action row. Use **Report** as the Object Type argument and **Late Tape Call List** as the Object Name argument.

3. Save the macro as **Print Late Tape Call List**. The macro window should look like Figure 4-13.

Figure 4-13

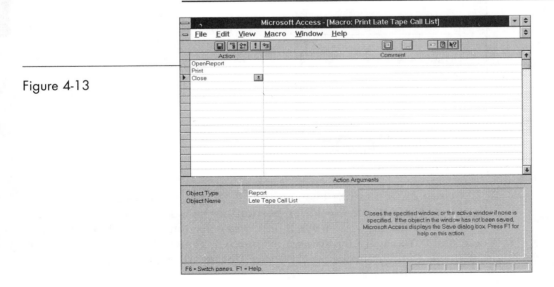

Running a Macro

A macro can be run from either the macro window or the database window. When used on a day-to-day basis, a macro is usually run from the database window. A common scenario would have an employee coming to work and assigned the job of calling customers with late tapes. The employee would then go to the nearest computer and follow a posted set of instructions to turn on the printer, choose on the Macros tab in the VIDSTORE database window, select Print Late Tape Call List, and click on the Run button. The report would automatically be printed and the screen display returned to the VIDSTORE database window. Let's try it!

■   Close the macro window.

▶   *The display returns to the VIDSTORE database window with the Print Late Tape Call List highlighted in the Macros list.*

■   Make sure the printer is on and ready to print.

■   Select the Run button.

▶   *Access displays the print message box with the print preview window in the background, prints the report, and returns the display to the VIDSTORE database window.*

USING PARAMETER QUERIES

Queries can be designed so you can change the search criteria each time a query is run. This type of query, called a **parameter query**, contains a prompt that asks you to enter a parameter Access uses when searching through the table. The prompt replaces the search criteria in the Criteria area of the QBE grid. Prompts are always enclosed in square brackets.

If the prompt [What rating?] is entered in the Rating Criteria area, as shown in Figure 4-14, Access will only include movies with the designated rating in the dynaset. The next time you run the query, you can enter another rating and Access will use it when creating the dynaset.

■   From the VIDSTORE database window, click on the Query tab, then select the New button, and choose the New Query button.

▶   *The Add Table dialog box is displayed.*

■   Add MOVIES, then close the Add Table dialog box.

▶   *The query design window opens.*

■   Place the following field names in the designated order into the Field area of the QBE grid: **Movie Title**, **Category**, **Rating**.

■   In the Rating Criteria area, type **[What rating?]**.

> ▶ *The QBE grid looks like Figure 4-14.*

■ Run the query.

> ▶ *The What Rating? prompt is displayed in the message box, as shown in Figure 4-14.*

■ Type **PG13** and press ENTER.

> ▶ *The dynaset includes at least three movies (see bottom of Figure 4-14).*

■ Return the display to the query design window.

Figure 4-14

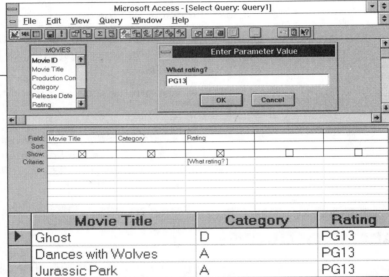

Queries can contain several prompts when desirable. For instance, it may be desirable to select movies by category as well as rating.

P R A C T I C E   T I M E   4 - 8

1. Add the prompt **[What Category (A, C, D, H, O, or S)?]** in the Category Criteria area. Do not be concerned if the prompt scrolls out of the Criteria area. If necessary, the LEFT ARROW and RIGHT ARROW keys can be used to move text back into the Criteria area.

2. Run the query for adventure (A) movies with a PG13 rating.

3. Return the display to the query design window.

Adding Tables to Query

From a practical point of view, this query is of limited use. While it identifies movies carried by the store that match the selection criteria, the user does not know if the movie is currently in the store and available for renting. The VIDSTORE database contains this information, but you need to add the INV table to the query.

■　From the Query menu, select Add Table.

Alternative:　Use the Add Table button, 🔳.

▶　*The Add Table dialog box opens.*

■　Add INV and close the Add Table dialog box.

▶　*The INV field list is added to the query design window with Movie ID serving as a link between the MOVIES and INV tables.*

■　Add **Tape Number** and **Available** to the QBE grid.

■　Run the query.

▶　*The prompt asks for a category.*

■　Type A for adventure movies and press ENTER.

▶　*Prompt asks for a rating.*

■　Type PG13 and press ENTER.

▶　*The dynaset displays at least four entries: two for Dances with Wolves and two for Jurassic Park.*

The video store carries several copies of popular movies. Since each tape has a unique tape number in the INV table, multiple copies of the same movie title are included in the dynaset when each tape number is listed.

When the Available field contains a *Y*, the movie is available for customer rentals. Damaged or destroyed tapes contain an *N* and are not available for renting. Notice that two of the four tapes are not available. However, we still do not know if the other tapes are currently in the store or if they have been rented.

To make this final determination, you need to add the RENTALS table to the query. The Date In field from this table will indicate whether the tape is in the store or not.

PRACTICE TIME 4-9

1. Return the display to the query design window.

2. Type **"Y"** into the Available Criteria area.

3. Add the RENTALS table to the query.

4. Place the **Date In** field name into the next available Field area of the QBE grid.

5. Save the query using **Available Movies** as a query name.

Figure 4-15

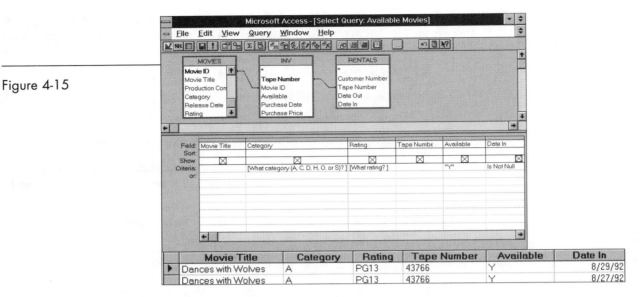

Using NOT in an Expression

Previously in the Late Tape Call List, you used the Date In field to determine if a tape was still out. In this situation the Date In field was blank, and the search criteria *Is Null* was used to identify rented tapes. In the Available Movies query, you want to identify the opposite situation, i.e., tapes that have been returned and are available for rental.

The NOT operator is used for this purpose. To identify Date In fields that have a return date and are not blank, you will use the criteria *Is Not Null*.

- ■   Type **is not null** into the Date In Criteria area.

  - ▶   *The QBE grid should look like the one in Figure 4-15.*

- ■   Run the query for adventure movies with a PG13 rating.

  - ▶   *Access displays a dynaset similar to the one in Figure 4-15.*

The dynaset in figure 4-15 tells you that Dances with Wolves tape number 43766 is available for renting. This movie is listed twice because the RENTALS table has two different dates; this is because the tape has been rented and returned two times. As a result, you might want to remove the Date In field from the QBE grid to avoid confusion.

- ■   Save the query.

- ■   Return the display to the VIDSTORE database window.

ENDING LESSON 4

Access is an extremely powerful software package that is designed to meet the needs of many people in a variety of situations. While this tutorial has only scratched the surface of many Access features, it has given you a valuable foundation from which to explore other features and capabilities. With time, patience, and a handy User's Guide, there is no limit to what you can do with this relational database management system.

This is the end of Lesson 4. Close all open windows and exit Access. If you are done with the computer, follow the recommended procedures for shutting down the computer system.

    ■   Close all open Access windows.

    ■   Exit Access.

SUMMARY

❑   **Data can be sorted in a query or within a table's datasheet view.**

❑   **Filters can be placed on a table's datasheet view to limit which records are displayed on the screen. These filters work just like a query's selection criteria.**

❑   **One-of-a-kind data displays from a single table are easily accomplished using filters. Recurring requests for up-to-date data from several tables are best handled and saved as a query.**

❑   **Indexing fields in a table can speed up sorting and searching, but may slow down data entry.**

❑   **An index is removed from a table using the indexes window and the Delete key while within the report design.**

❑   **Two tables are automatically joined together as they are added to a multi-table query when one table has a primary key field that also occurs in the other table.**

❑   **Referential integrity is maintained by not allowing a record with a primary key field to be deleted while joined with records in other tables.**

❑   **Special functions like Now( ) and reserved words like Null are available to enhance query development.**

❑   **The Expression Builder window helps users create a field in a table, query, or form that is based on a formula.**

❑   **The AutoReport Wizard automatically creates a report using the single-column format and the highlighted table or query.**

❑   **The macro window allows users to select a set of Access commands that combine to automate repetitious tasks with Access.**

DATABASE

❑   **A parameter query is designed to allow users to change the search criteria each time the query is run.**

❑   **Tables are easily joined in multiple-table queries using the Add Table button in the tool bar.**

KEY TERMS

filter   macro   parameter query
index   module   referential integrity
join line   null

COMMAND SUMMARY

Records
Quick Sort
Edit Filter/Sort
Apply Filter/Sort
Show All Records

View
Indexes

Query
Add Table

REVIEW QUESTIONS

1. When do you create and save a query instead of manipulating data within a table's datasheet?

2. How is a query different from a filter, and how do you turn off a filter?

3. What are the advantages and disadvantages to indexing fields in a table?

4. How do you manually create a join line that connects two tables in a query?

5. Describe a situation using the CUSTOMER and RENTAL tables where referential integrity would be lost.

6. How does Access treat dates?

7. How is the Expression Builder window used?

8. Given that a dynaset or table with the desired data already exists, what is the easiest way to create a single-column report using these data?

9. Identify six different types of Access objects.

10. How are commands added to a macro?

11. How is a parameter query different from a standard select query?

12. How do you add a table to an open query design window?

EXERCISES

1. Reorganize your personal information in the FRIENDS table of the PERSONAL database.
   a. Create and print mailing labels for each friend. The mailing label should include the name, address, city, state/prov, and zip/postal code in a format that is acceptable to the Post Office.
   b. Index the birthday field (Duplicates are OK.).
   c. Create a query called **Birthday List**, that includes the name, complete address, telephone, and birthday of everyone in the FRIENDS table. Sort the dynaset in ascending order by birthday.
   d. Prepare and print a report called **Birthday List** using the Birthday List query. The report should include the following headings:
      BIRTHDAYS BY MONTH   **Today's Date**
      The report's detail section must use the following data: Name, Address, Telephone, Birthday (mm/dd/yy format). Include a count of how many names are in the list. Hint: Use the =count ([field name]) function to count birthdays or names.
   e. Create a macro called **Print Birthday List** that automatically opens the Birthday List report, prints it, and then closes the report.

2. Update the STOCKS table in the BUSINESS database, create a new Groups/Total report, and a parameter query.
   a. Add at least four new transactions to the STOCKS table. Each purchase should be of a stock you currently own.
   b. Index the Stock Name field (Duplicates are OK.).
   c. Quick Sort the STOCKS table by Stock Name and print the table as a datasheet.
   d. Create and print a Groups/Total report called **Stocks by Company** that groups stocks by Stock Name and provides a total number of shares for each group. A grand total is not necessary. The detail section should include the following: Transaction Number, Number of Shares, Purchase Price, and Date Purchased. The report heading should include your name and today's date in the following format:
      Your Name's STOCK HOLDINGS BY COMPANY Today's Date
   e. Create a macro called **Print Stocks by Company** that automatically opens the Stocks by Company report, prints it, and then closes the report.
   f. Create a parameter query called **Selected Stocks** that allows the user to select a stock name for the search criteria. The dynaset should include all the fields associated with the STOCKS table. Print a dynaset with data about your favorite stock.

3. Restructure the INV table in the STUDENT database, create a new report based on a two-table query.
   a. Index the Supplier Name field in the SUPPLIER table (no duplicates).

b. Quick Sort the SUPPLIER table by Supplier Number and print sorted table as a datasheet.

c. Modify the table design of the INV table by adding a Supplier Number field (text, 6 characters).

d. Add Supplier Numbers to the INV table using Supplier Numbers from the SUPPLIER table.

e. Create a three-table query called **Reorder Movies** using the SUPPLIER, INV, and MOVIES tables. The Supplier Number links the SUPPLIER and INV tables. The Movie Id links the INV and MOVIES tables. The dynaset is limited to records where *Available = N*, sorted in ascending order by Supplier Name, and includes the following fields: Supplier Name, complete mailing address, Telephone, Movie Title, and Purchase Price.

f. Modify the Reorder Movies as a parameter query and save it as **Reorder Movies by Supplier**. This query should include a prompt that allows the user to select which Supplier Number is included in the related dynaset. Print the dynaset with reorder data from the supplier of your choice.

g. Prepare and print a Groups/Total report called **Reorder Movies** which is based on the Reorder Movies query. The report should group records by Supplier Name, lists the Movie Title and Purchase Price in the detail section, and provides the total purchase price for each supplier along with a grand total of all the purchase prices. Add the telephone number field under the supplier's name in the group header. Change properties to align fields and labels.

h. Create a macro called **Print Reorder Movies** that automatically opens the Reorder Movies report, prints it, and then closes the report.

i. Create another macro that automatically runs the Reorder Movies by Supplier query.

Access Projects

PROJECT 1: QUICK PIC FILM DEVELOPMENT

Quick Pic is an overnight film processing service. The company uses a database management system to track the film that customers drop off for processing.

This project uses the CUSTOMER table on your data disk.

1. Create a new database called QUICKPIC.

2. Attach the CUSTOMER table from the STUDENT database to the QUICKPIC database.

3. Create a new table called FILM with the following fields:

   Field 1 - Envelope Number, text, 6 characters, primary key

   Field 2 - Date In, Date

   Field 3 - Customer Number, text, 6 characters

   Field 4 - Film Type, text, 4 characters

   Field 5 - Exposure, number

   Field 6 - Format, text, 1 character

   Field 7 - Date Back, date

   Field 8 - Date Pickup, date

2. Create a data entry form for the FILM table. The form includes the following header: **QUICK PIC Film Development**.

3. Enter the following data into the FILM table using the data entry form:

Env. No.	Date In	Cust. No.	Type	Exp.	Fmt.	Date Back	Date Pickup
101	10/15/94	94111	35	24	C	10/16/94	10/17/94
102	10/15/94	886951	35	36	C	10/16/94	
103	10/15/94	894239	DISC	24	C	10/16/94	10/16/94
104	10/16/94	927494	110	12	C	10/17/94	10/20/94
105	10/16/94	881464	35	36	S	10/17/94	10/17/94
106	10/16/94	881464	35	36	S		
107	10/17/94	915968	35	24	B	10/20/94	
108	10/17/94	884317	110	24	C	10/18/94	10/19/94
109	10/17/94	922232	DISC	24	C	10/18/94	10/20/94

4. Right-align the Film Type field data and center the Format field data in the datasheet.

5. Create a two-table query using the CUSTOMER and FILM tables. The query creates a dynaset that lists customers who have film back and not picked up, which means there is no date in the Date Pickup field.

   Hint: The Date Back field must be greater than 1/1/94 to exclude any film not yet processed.

   Print the dynaset as a datasheet with each customer's name and telephone number along with the envelope number and the date the film came in.

6. Create and print mailing labels for customers with film to pick up. The mailing label must include the customer's full name, street address, city, state/province, zip/postal code.

7. Develop and print a group/total report called **Daily Film Processing** that lists by date the film type, format, and exposure. Use the following guidelines in creating the report.
   a. The report heading should include **Prepared by** *your name* and the date.
   b. The page header identifies the Film Type, Exposure, and Format.
   c. The page footer contains the page number.
   d. The group footer includes a count of the rolls of film processed each day.
   e. The detail section includes the fields Film Type, Exposure, and Format. Align these fields under the related labels in the page header.

8. Create a macro that automatically opens, prints, then closes the Daily Film Processing report.

PROJECT 2: MAGAZINES US

Magazines US is a telemarketing magazine subscription service. The company uses a database management system to track customer subscriptions and telemarketer sales performance.

This project uses the CUSTOMER table from your data disk.

1. Create a new database called SUBSCRIB.

2. Attach the CUSTOMER table from the STUDENT database to the SUBSCRIB database.

3. Create two new tables: MAGAZINE and SALES.

NOTE: The SALES table has a multiple-field primary key, Customer Number + ISS Number. This is accomplished by holding the Ctrl key to highlight both fields before selecting the primary key button.

MAGAZINE

Field 1 - ISS Number, text, 9 characters, primary key

Field 2 - Magazine Name, text, 30 characters

Field 3 - Price, currency

Field 4 - Issues per Year, number

SALES

Field 1 - Customer Number, text, 6 characters, primary key

Field 2 - ISS Number, text, 9 characters, primary key

Field 3 - Date of Sale, Date

Field 4 - Renewal, Yes/No

Field 5 - Sales Rep ID, text, 4 characters

4. Create a data entry form for each table. Each form has the heading MAGAZINES US and an appropriate form identification.

5. Enter the following data into the tables using the data entry forms.

MAGAZINE Table

Issue No.	Magazine Name	Price	Issues per Yr.
0163-6626	Interface	14.00	4
0192-592X	THE Journal	29.00	12
0278-3258	Electronic Learning	23.95	8
0740-1604	PC Week	160.00	52
0888-8507	PC Magazine	44.97	24

Issue No.	Magazine Name	Price	Issues per Yr.
1040-6484	PC Today	24.00	12
1058-7071	Access News	44.95	12
1060-7188	New Media	48.00	12

SALES Table

Cust. No.	ISS No.	Date of Sale	Renew	Sales Rep ID
881464	1060-7188	10/6/94	N	5438
894239	0740-1604	10/7/94	N	5438
894239	0888-8507	10/7/94	N	5438
897062	1040-6484	10/7/94	Y	1432
913271	1058-7071	10/6/94	N	1432
923843	0278-3258	10/5/94	Y	1432
927494	0192-592X	10/6/94	Y	9540
929655	0163-6626	10/5/94	Y	5438
929655	0192-592X	10/5/94	N	5438
929655	0278-3258	10/5/94	Y	5438
941111	1058-7071	10/5/94	N	9540

6. Create a three-table query using the CUSTOMER, MAGAZINE, and SALES tables. The query creates a dynaset that shows customer information on all purchases from sales representative 5438 where the magazine name starts with the letters PC.

   Print the dynaset as a datasheet containing the magazine name, customer name, and sales rep. ID.

7. Develop and print a group/total report called **Sales by Renewal Status** that groups data by renewal status. Use the following guidelines in creating the report.
   a. The report heading should include **MAGAZINES US**, *your name*, and the *date*.
   b. Sort records by renewal status, then ISS Number.
   c. The page header identifies the ISS Number, Date of Sale, Sales Rep Number, and Customer Number.
   d. The page footer contains the page number.
   e. The group footer includes a count of the number of renewals in each group.
   f. The detail section includes the fields ISS Number, Date of Sale, Sales Rep Number, and Customer Number. Align these fields under the

related labels in the page header.

8. Create a report based on a two-table query that uses the MAGAZINE and SALES tables. The query should include date of sale, ISS number, and price. Sort the dynaset by date of sale. The group/total report should include the following:

   a. Customized report header:

   MAGAZINES US Daily Sales Report
   prepared by *your name*

   b. Detail section and related page header that display ISS Number and Price fields.

   c. Group band based on Date of Sale field.

   d. Add a calculated field that sums daily sales at the bottom of the group band. Label this field Daily Sales Total.

9. Create macros that automatically open, print, then close the Sales by renewal report and the Daily Sales report.

Access Command Summary

This section is a quick reference for the Microsoft's Access for Windows commands covered in this manual. This is *not* a complete list of all Access commands.   -
     ... indicates a dialog box will open

Task	Menu Command	Alternative
DATABASE COMMANDS		
Create a new database	File - New Database...	Ctrl+N
Open an existing database	File - Open Database...	Ctrl+O or 🖼
Close database	File - Close Database	
Create new database object	File - New	
Table	Table	
Query	Query	🖼
Form	Form	
Report	Report	🖼
Macro	Macro	
Module	Module	
Rename database	File - Rename...	
Import data from another database	File - Import...	
Export data in another database format	File - Export...	
Attach data from another database	File - Attach...	
Edit import/export specifications	File - Imp/Exp Setup...	
Exit the Access database window	File - Exit	Alt+F4
View list of tables in database	View - Table	
View list of queries in database	View - Query	
View list of forms in database	View - Form	
View list of reports in database	View - Report	
View list of macros in database	View - Macro	
WINDOW COMMANDS		
Display all open windows side by side	Window - Tile	
Overlap all open windows	Window - Cascade	

Task	Menu Command	Alternative
HELP COMMANDS		
Display Help table of contents	Help - Contents	🔲
Search for information in Help or Cue Cards	Help - Search...	
Display online couch for designated task	Help - Cue Cards	
EDITING COMMANDS		
Undo last operation	Edit - Undo	Ctrl+Z
Cut current selection to Clipboard	Edit - Cut	Ctrl+X
Copy current selection to Clipboard	Edit - Copy	Ctrl+C
Paste Clipboard contents	Edit - Paste	Ctrl+V
Delete selection without copying to Clipboard	Edit - Delete	Del
Find specified text	Edit - Find	Ctrl+F
Find and replace specified text	Edit - Replace	Ctrl+H
OBJECT-ORIENTED COMMANDS		
Create a new database object	File - New	
Close active window	File - Close	
Save active object	File - Save	Ctrl+S or 🔲
Save active object with new name	File - Save As	
Select printer or change printer settings	File - Print Setup...	
Preview printed output	File - Print Preview	🔲
Print a file	File - Print...	Ctrl+P or 🔲
Select current record	Edit - Select Record	
Select all records	Edit - Select All Records	Ctrl+A
Change font type, size, or style	Format - Font...	
Set height of selected row	Format - Row Height...	
Set width of selected column	Format - Column Width...	
RECORD COMMANDS		
Move record selector	Records - Goto	
go to first record	First	
go to previous record	Previous	
go to next record	Next	
go to last record Last		
new record New		
Sort records	Records - Quick Sort	
in ascending order	Ascending	🔲
in descending order	Descending	🔲
Specify filter or sort criteria	Records - Edit Filter/Sort...	🔲
Apply filter or sort criteria	Records - Apply Filter/Sort	🔲
Remove filter and display underlying records	Records - Show All Records	🔲
Allow changes or prevent changes to data	Records - Allow Editing	

DATABASE

Task	Menu Command	Alternative
TABLE COMMANDS		
Create a new table	File - New	
Save active record	File - Save Record	Shift+Enter
Insert row above selected row	Edit - Insert Row	
Delete selected row	Edit - Delete Row	
Designate selected column(s) as the key	Edit - Set Primary Key	
Display the table in Design view	View - Table Design	⊞
Display the table as a datasheet	View - Datasheet	⊞
View and edit indexes	View - Indexes...	
Turn gridlines on or off	Format - Gridlines	
FORM COMMANDS		
Create a new form	File - New	
Display the form in Design view	View - Form Design	⊞
Display the form	View - Form	⊞
Display as a datasheet	View - Datasheet	⊞
Open or close list of fields	View - Filed List...	⊞
Set form properties	View - Properties...	⊞
Show or hide ruler	View - Ruler	
Show or hide grid	View - Grid	
Open or close toolbox	View - Toolbox	
Open or close palette	View - Palette	
Turn control Wizard on or off	View - Control Wizard	
QUERY COMMANDS		
Create a new query	File - New	⊞
Run query	Query - Run	!
Add new table to query	Query - Add Table	⊞
Clear contents of QBE grid	Edit - Clear Grid	
Insert row before selected row in QBE grid	Edit - Insert Row	
Delete row before selected row of QBE grid	Edit - Delete Row	
Insert column to left of selected grid column	Edit - Insert Column	
Delete selected column in grid	Edit - Delete Column	
Display the query in Design view	View - Query Design	⊞
Display the query's dynaset	View - Datasheet	⊞
Set query properties	View - Properties...	⊞
Turn gridlines on or off	Format - Gridlines	
REPORT COMMANDS		
Create a new report	File - New	⊞
Open or close list of fields	View - Field List...	⊞
Set form properties	View - Properties...	⊞

Show or hide ruler	<u>V</u>iew - <u>R</u>uler
Show or hide grid	<u>V</u>iew - <u>G</u>rid
Open or close toolbox	<u>V</u>iew - <u>T</u>oolbox
Open or close palette	<u>V</u>iew - P<u>a</u>lette
Turn control Wizard on or off	<u>V</u>iew - Control <u>W</u>izard

MACRO COMMANDS

Create a new macro	<u>F</u>ile - <u>N</u>ew	
Execute macro commands	<u>F</u>ile - R<u>u</u>n Macro	
	<u>M</u>acro - <u>R</u>un	

Glossary

alphanumeric   Data that includes both uppercase and lowercase letters, numbers, and symbols.

attaching   Linking a table to a database without changing its native format.

button   Labeled icon that confirms or cancels some program option.

click   To press a mouse button once to select a menu option or icon.

column separator   Vertical line found between column headers. The column separator can be dragged to the left or right in order to adjust the width of the related column.

comparison operators   Operators, like greater than or less than, that are used to describe data ranges as part of a query's or filter's selection criterion.

complex queries   Queries with multiple selection criteria which incorporate the local operators AND/OR.

context-sensitive help   Information supplied by the help window that changes based on the Access feature currently being used.

cursor   Blinking line or box that highlights where the computer will display the next keyboard entry.

data   Facts, figures, and images.

database management system (DBMS)   Software tool that permits people to use a computer's ability to store, retrieve, modify, organize, and display key facts.

datasheet   Row/column format used to display multiple records at the same time.

detail section   Body of a report that contains the fields from the underlying table or query.

dialog box   Window that prompts the user to enter text, select names from a list, or click on an icon to initiate or cancel some program option.

disk directory   Storage area on a disk that contains the filename, size, date, and time of each data file or program saved on the disk.

disk operating system (DOS)   Collection of system software designed to control a computer system using disks for storage.

double-click   To press a mouse button twice in quick succession to run a program or activate a program operation.

drop-down menu (pull-down menu)   Menu options that stay hidden in a menu bar at the top of the screen until the user selects a menu. When the menu is selected, the menu opens to list program options. Once an option is selected, the menu rolls back up into the menu bar.

dynaset   Special view of data from one or more tables that is filtered through a query.

ellipsis   Series of three periods. When found behind a menu option, an ellipsis indicates that additional user input is necessary when using that option.

error message   Screen display that is a result of the computer's failure to function properly or is a warning of a potential problem.

exclusive   Only one user at a time can access designated database.

expression   Identifies the criteria Access uses to add data to a query's dynaset or a table's datasheet display.

field   Combination of characters that represents a single fact.

field name   Generic name given to a data field.

filename   Unique set of letters, numbers, and symbols that identifies a data file or program.

filename extension   A combination of three letters preceded by a period that is added to the end of a filename to identify the file format.

filter   Criteria used to selectively display data.

form   Display format which is limited to fields associated with a single record.

function   Built-in code that performs a specific task, like pagination or statistical computation, and places results where function name is located.

graphical user interface (GUI)   Interface that relies on mouse or keyboard input to select menus or icons that initiate program options.

help screen   Description of software features and explanation of error messages displayed upon demand so the user does not have to refer to a manual.

icon   Picture representing an item, action, or computer operation.

index   An index is used to speed up sorting of records and searching for data in a table. Adding too many indexes to a table could result in slowing down data entry.

import   Linking a table to a database by converting it into the new database's native format.

join field   Field common to two or more tables that Access uses to combine data from both tables into a single dynaset.

join line   Line designating a link between two tables. The line is drawn to connect the field both tables have in common.

jump term   Underlined word or phrase in a help window which references additional help. Double-clicking on the term activates the additional help.

key   Field that uniquely identifies a record.

keyboard   Input hardware containing typewriter-like keys that the user presses.

label box   Displays descriptive data. Label boxes are used for titles and column headings.

landscape   Page orientation that is wider than it is tall.

launch (execute)   To start the execution of a computer program.

list box   Displays a list of names or options. When the list is too long to fit in the box, scroll arrows move the list up and down to display different items within the list box.

logical operators   The AND and OR operators used in complex queries.

macro   Set of Access commands that automate routine or repetitive tasks.

module   Complete computer program written in Access native command language.

move handle   Appears in top left corner of label or text box when it is active. Dragging move handle to a new location in the report repositions the box in the report output.

navigation buttons   Set of four icons found above the status bar that are used to move the selector to the first, previous, next, or last record or page.

null   An empty field.

numeric data   Data containing only numbers (0–9), decimal point, and plus (+) and negative (-) signs.

object   Basic building block of an Access database which includes tables, forms, queries, and reports.

page footer   The bottom of each report page. The page footer could contain custom labels, page number, or date.

page header   The top of each report page. The page header could contain column labels, page numbers, or date.

parameter query   Query designed to let user change search condition every time the query is run.

pointer   Marker that indicates the active record in a table.

portrait   Page orientation that is taller than it is wide.

primary key   Field used by Access to organize and identify a record.

printer   Output hardware that produces information on paper.

property sheet   Lists default report settings.

query   Question user asks concerning database data which is in a format that prompts Access to display selected data.

record   Collection of related fields about a single person, place, object, or event.

record selector   Black triangle that identifies the active record in a table.

referential integrity   Fields that join tables in a relational database are not deleted as long as links to other tables still exist.

relational database   Integrated tables that can be accessed at the same time by a database management system.

report footer   Last part of a report. In long reports the report footer would contain references and possible footnotes.

report header   First part of a report. In long reports the report header would contain a title page and table of contents.

screen pointer   Onscreen icon, usually an arrow, that

DATABASE

moves when the mouse or some other pointer device is moved. Program options are activated using a mouse by moving the screen pointer over the desired icon and clicking the mouse button.

scroll To roll onscreen data up, down, or sideways for viewing long or wide documents.

scroll arrows Arrows found at either end of a scroll bar. Users change the view of a window or list box by clicking on one of the scroll arrows.

scroll bar Area that appears on the right or lower edge of a window or list box when only a partial view is available. A scroll bar contains a scroll box and scroll arrows.

scroll box Square within a scroll bar that identifies which portion of the window or list box is currently being viewed. Users can change the view by dragging the scroll box within the scroll bar.

select query Allows users to selectively view data based on the specified criteria.

sizing handles These boxes and connecting lines appear when a label or text is active. Dragging handle to a new report location changes the display size of the box.

status bar Area at the bottom of a window where Access displays field descriptions.

table Group of related records.

table design Information about the contents of a table which includes field names, data types, date entry descriptions, and field formats.

text box Displays data from designated table or query.

tool bar Area beneath the menu bar in an Access application window which contains tool buttons.

tool button Icon found in the tool bar. Clicking on a tool button activates a commonly used program command. Using a tool button is an alternative to using a drop-down menu.

updating Adding, changing, or deleting data.

wildcard character Symbol used to represent any combination of characters.

window Subdivides a screen display to allow the user to look at several menus, dialog boxes, or status reports from more than one program.

wizard Special utility that helps users design database objects by automating common procedures.

working disk drive Disk drive with disk and related directory containing desired Access database.

Index

DATABASE